THE OFFICIAL ITV SPORT

WORLD CUP 06 FACT FILE

ORDEM E PROG

THE OFFICIAL ITV SPORT

WORLD CUP 06 FACT FILE

Keir Radnedge

CARLTON BOOKS

THE OFFICIAL ITV SPORT WORLD CUP
06 FACT FILE

First published by Carlton Books 2006

A CIP catalogue record of this book is available upon request.

ISBN 1 84442 322 0

Editor: Nigel Matheson
Art Director: Luke Griffin
Designer: Ben Ruocco
Picture Research: Tom Wright
Production: Lisa French

Carlton Books Limited
20 Mortimer Street
London W1T 3JW

Printed and bound in the UK

Carlton Books

Publisher's note
All match times in this book are British Summer Time.

CONTENTS

Fußball-Woche

INTRODUCTION

THE GREATEST SHOW ON EARTH

At last... the qualifying rounds are wrapped up and the draw's showbiz kitsch tidied away. Now the pitches of 12 magnificent stadia are being thrown wide open for the 32 finalists of the 18th World Cup to write their own sporting history upon.

Brazil enter the finals as probably heavier favourites than at any previous World Cup. By contrast, fewer than 20 per cent of Germans believe the host nation can carry off the FIFA World Cup for the fourth time and for the first time since reunification.

The honour of appearing, never mind winning, the World Cup is one thing; the money generated is something else – both a record and a consolation for the 31 nations whose players will not laugh, cry, pray and turn somersaults of delight at the climactic final whistle in Berlin's redeveloped Olympic stadium on July 9.

The winners will carry off 24.5m Swiss francs (£11.2m), the runners-up Swf22.55m (£10.3m) and the semi-finalists Swf21.5m (£9.8m) apiece – twice as much as each of the losing quarter-finalists. Second-round losers will take home Swf8.55m (£3.9m). The first-round guarantee is a minimum of Swf7m (£3.2m) made up of Swf1m (£456,000) towards preparatory costs and a further Swf2m (£913,000) each for every first-round match.

FIFA's largesse knows few golden bounds. The world federation bears the travel costs of each delegation up to a maximum of 45 people plus partial costs for accommodation.

DROP IN THE OCEAN

But the game's rulers have also bowed to pressure stirred up by Europe's top clubs, notably through the G-14 group. For the first time FIFA has set up an insurance policy to cover all participating players against serious injury. Around Swf15m (£6.8m) has been set aside for premiums – which still represents a mere drop in the ocean of Swf300m (£136m) set aside to cover costs.

The awards schedule is headed by the Golden Ball for the top player, the Golden Boot for the top scorer and silver and bronze awards for the players placed second and third in both categories. A man of the match prize will be awarded after every game, the Lev Yashin prize for the best goalkeeper and fans will be polled on the most entertaining team.

GLITTERING PRIZES

A fair play prize will again combine assessments of the behaviour of players, officials and fans, while a new trophy will reward the best young player from among those starlets born on, or after, January 1, 1985.

Even the World Cup trophy has been put to work to fire the passion of fans worldwide ahead of its unveiling at the opening match between hosts Germany and Costa Rica in Munich on June 9. The 18-carat, solid-gold symbol of world supremacy has been undertaking a world tour of its own to all the finalist nations.

The cup has even been renovated back in its Milan birthplace by Silvio Gazzaniga, whose original design was chosen out of the 53 submitted to FIFA after Brazil gained possession of the original Jules Rimet trophy with their third triumph in 1970. The FIFA World Cup is one of the smallest trophies in the game, standing only 36.8cm (14.5ins) high on its malachite plinth, but it remains the most valuable of all.

The 2002 final, in which Brazil beat Germany 2–0, was watched by 1.1billion fans worldwide, while the total audience of 28.8billion for the co-hosted drama in Korea and Japan far outstripped comparative figures for the Athens Olympic Games two years later. FIFA's own website went down in history as the most successful sports portal in history with 2.34billion hits.

But the statistics are only an appropriate fraction of the story. The World Cup finals endure on a legacy of passion and drama, thrills and controversy, brilliance and blunders . . . and, of course, goals.

CHANGED DAYS

The 2006 finals would be unrecognisable for Rimet and his fellow pioneering officials and players who launched the World Cup in Uruguay when the world was a very different place back in 1930.

At that time, there were no sponsors, no television and most of the players were amateurs or, at the least, part-timers. FIFA then boasted only a few dozen members, a far cry from today's 207 drawn from the icy floes of the north seas to the sunny shores of the southern Pacific.

But that is progress and the German setting promises the most feverish World Cup yet with the demand for tickets having far outstripped supply. Organising president Franz Beckenbauer says: "We had 'only' around 3 million tickets, but if we'd had 10 million it would not have been enough in Germany alone, let alone the rest of the world."

That is the power and glory of the World Cup.

© 2002 FIFA TM
FIFA WORLD CUP
GERMANY
2006

THE DRAW

OUT OF THE HAT

Leipzig unrolled the longest red carpet in history to welcome the World Cup. The plush 2,200 metres were unrolled in honour of the footballing royalty who descended on the city for the finals draw on December 9 last year.

"The virtual kick-off to the World Cup," as organising president Franz Beckenbauer put it, was played out to a live audience of 4,500, including the new German Chancellor Angela Merkel, plus 320 million watching on television in 150 countries around the world.

Leipzig was chosen for two reasons. Firstly, Leipzig is the only city from the former East Germany figuring among the host venues, so this provided a further opportunity to underline the reunification message. Secondly, Leipzig in 1900 was the birthplace of the Deutscher Fussball-Bund. Selection thus neatly linked two of the most significant dates in German football history.

Back in 1974, when the DFB last welcomed the world, barely 200 journalists were present at the draw. This time 2,000 registered for a celebrity-studded show, mixing football with the illusionist skills of Dutch magician Hans Klok and the energy of Colombian rock star Juanes.

But the applause was edged with impatience. The celebrities who mattered were eight golden oldies, headed by Germany's Lothar Matthaus, Cameroon's Roger Milla, Holland's Johan Cruyff and the inimitable Pele.

No more illusions. This time it was for real when the famous four helped pluck 32 mini-footballs from their glass shells to determine the fate of nations. Each successive "hatching" represented a further layer of logistical options and visions of glory.

Plastered across the walls of the congress centre, in English, was the World Cup logo: "A time to make friends". Beckenbauer says: "I can't imagine a better slogan. We're inviting the fans to join us in celebrating a joyful World Cup."

But the inevitable consequences of the draw will mean ultimate joy for only one of the 32 contenders who trod Leipzig's red carpet 182 days before the real kick-off.

LEFT: Heidi Klum, new German President Horst Kohler, FIFA President Sepp Blatter and German moderator Reinhold Beckman before the draw.

BELOW: Johan Cruyff keeps a wary eye on Pele as the great Brazilian picks a ball from the glass bowl.

PREVIEW: THE STADIA

Twelve new and magnificently redeveloped stadia will welcome the world to the 2006 finals. For eight of the cities this will not be a new experience. Berlin, Dortmund, Frankfurt, Gelsenkirchen, Hamburg, Hanover, Munich and Stuttgart were all involved as hosts when the Federal Republic of West Germany – as it then was – staged the World Cup back in 1974.

The one city dropped from the 1974 list is Dusseldorf. Newcomers are Cologne, Kaiserslautern, Leipzig and Nuremberg. Leipzig is the only city from the former East Germany chosen as a host.

Otherwise – and setting aside the unique status of pre-unification Berlin, marooned inside the GDR – all the other cities in 1974 were situated geographically within the former West Germany.

However, only six of the current stadia – and all of them now redeveloped beyond recognition – were involved 32 years ago. Fans in two other cities – Gelsenkirchen and Munich – now watch their football in different homes entirely.

In 1974 matches in Gelsenkirchen in the heart of the Ruhr were staged in the Parkstadion; now that vast bowl stands in the shadow of the new Arena AufSchalke which opened its big-event doors for the first time for the 2004 UEFA Champions League final in which Porto beat Monaco 3–0.

Munich, 32 years ago, hosted five matches, including the third-place play-off and the final in which hosts West Germany beat Holland 2–1. But the specific venue was the iconic Olympic stadium which had been the heart of the ill-starred Games of two years earlier.

By the mid-1990s, however, it was becoming clear that the demands of modern soccer had outgrown this remarkable stadium, with its spider-web roof, its long-distance sight lines and restrictive architectural covenants.

Thus Bayern and neighbours TSV 1860, who rented and shared it, decided to move out and build their own new home which was opened last year. The new stadium – so far advanced technologically it can change colour depending on whether Bayern (red) or 1860 (blue) are playing at home – will thus welcome the glitz and glamour surrounding the opening match.

The proud boast of German organizing

1. HAMBURG

- Fixtures:
  10 June: ARG v IVO 20.00 [C]
  15 June: ECU v COS 14.00 [A]
  19 June: SAU v UKR 17.00 [H]
  22 June: CZE v ITA 15.00 [E]
  30 June: quarter-final
- Tournament name: FIFA World Cup Stadium
- Bundesliga name: AOL Arena also Volksparkstadion
- Capacity: 45,442 (non-WC 55,000)
- Cost: €97million
- Car parking: 10,000
- Transport: car, bus
- 1974 World Cup: three matches (including East Germany 1, West Germany 0)

Club: Hamburg SV (Bundesliga)

The city (pop. 1.7million): Hamburg, on the Elbe, is Germany's largest port and the country's second-biggest city after Berlin. It was founded by Emperor Charlemagne in 810 and composers Brahms and Mendelssohn were born there. The 1960s centre-forward Uwe Seeler is among the city's most popular modern sons.

2. HANOVER (HANNOVER)

- Fixtures:
  12 June: ITA v GHA 20.00 [E]
  16 June: MEX v ANG 20.00 [D]
  20 June: COS v POL 15.00 [A]
  23 June: SWI v KOR 20.00 [G]
  27 June: second-round match
- Tournament name: FIFA World Cup Stadium
- Bundesliga name: AWD-Arena also Niedersachsenstadion
- Capacity: 39,197 (non-WC 48,646)
- Cost: €63million
- Car parking: 6,000
- Transport: car, bus, rail
- 1974 World Cup: four matches

Club: Hannover 96 (Bundesliga)

The city (pop. 525,000): Hanover is the capital of Lower Saxony (Niedersachsen) and one of the Electors (princes) of the city became England's King George I in 1714. It has attained a worldwide reputation through its international industrial trade fair – though the local football club has yet to achieve such status.

3. BERLIN

- Fixtures:
  13 June: BRA v CRO 20.00 [F]
  15 June: SWE v PAR 20.00 [B]
  20 June: ECU v GER 15.00 [A]
  23 June: UKR v TUN 15.00 [H]
  30June: quarter-final
  9 July: final
- Tournament name: Olympiastadion
- Bundesliga name: Olympiastadion
- Capacity: 66,021 (non-WC 74,176)
- Cost: €242million
- Car parking: 5,415
- Transport: car, metro, tram, park-and-ride
- 1974 World Cup: three matches

Club: Hertha Berlin (Bundesliga)

The city (pop. 3.4million): Founded over 1,000 years ago on the banks of the river Spree, Berlin became the capital of the original united Germany in 1871. It was the site of the world's first motorway, the Avus Autobahn opened in 1921, and hosted the controversial 1936 Olympic Games. It was then divided between the four allies at the end of the Second World War in 1945. The collapse of the Berlin Wall, erected by the communist regime, led directly to the reunification of Germany and Berlin's reinstatement as capital.

4. GELSENKIRCHEN

- Fixtures:
  9 June: POL v ECU 20.00 [A]
  12 June: USA v CZE 17.00 [E]
  16 June: ARG v SER 14.00 [C]
  21 June: POR v MEX 15.00 [D]
  1 July: quarter-final
- Tournament name: Arena AufSchalke
- Bundesliga name: Veltins-Arena also Arena AufSchalke
- Capacity: 48,426 (non-WC 61,524)
- Cost: €192million
- Car parking: 21,000
- Transport: car, bus, rail
- 1974 World Cup: not built

Club: Schalke 04 (Bundesliga)

The city (pop. 278,000): Gelsenkirchen is a former coal-mining centre in the Ruhr 20 miles west of Dortmund. Local club Schalke dominated German football in the 1930s. The stadium was the first built in Germany with not only a sliding roof but a sliding pitch which sits outside the stadium in between matches.

5. DORTMUND

- Fixtures:
  10 June: TRI v SWE 17.00 [B]
  14 June: GER v POL 20.00 [A]
  19 June: TOG v SWI 14.00 [G]
  22 June: JAP v BRA 20.00 [F]
  27 June: second-round match
  4 July: semi-final
- Tournament name: Westfalenstadion
- Bundesliga name: Westfalenstadion
- Capacity: 60,285 (non-WC 83,000)
- Cost: €36million
- Car parking: 9,000
- Transport: car, bus, tram
- 1974 World Cup: four matches

Club: Borussia Dortmund (Bundesliga)

The city (pop. 590,000): Dortmund is the second-largest city of the industrial Ruhr after neighbouring Essen. For years it was the largest producer of beer and boasted one of the country's biggest steel plants. The Westfalenstadion was built for the 1974 World Cup behind the original Rote Erde stadium.

6. LEIPZIG

- Fixtures:
  11 June: SER v HOL14.00 [C]
  14 June: SPA v UKR 14.00 [H]
  18 June: FRA v KOR 20.00 [G]
  21 June: IRA v ANG 15.00 [D]
  24 June: second-round match
- Tournament name: Zentralstadion
- Bundesliga name: Zentralstadion
- Capacity: 38,898 (non-WC 45,000)
- Cost: €90.6million
- Car parking: 5,500
- Transport: car, tram, park-and-ride
- 1974 World Cup: not eligible (then East Germany)

Club: Sachsen Leipzig (Oberliga-Sud, a regional league)

The city (pop. 494,000): Leipzig is the one former East German city involved in the World Cup. Once described as "Paris in miniature", it used to be the cultural heart of Germany through religious reformer Martin Luther and poets Johann Goethe and Johann Schiller. Composer Richard Wagner was born in Leipzig.

committee president Franz Beckenbauer is that all 12 stadia were "World Cup fit" a year before the finals. Or, at least, as fit as possible in the circumstances. Beckenbauer and his aides had the opportunity to demonstrate the fact by using five of the chosen venues during the Confederations Cup in June 2005.

Cologne, Nuremberg, Leipzig and Hanover were put to the FIFA test along with Frankfurt, which staged the final in which Brazil met Argentina, possibly a taste of things to come in 2006.

The importance of the test was demonstrated by a number of security glitches and the embarrassment of seeing the vendor kiosks run out of beer by half-time at the opening match, also in Frankfurt. Beckenbauer duly assured Sepp Blatter, president of world governing body FIFA, that any such issues would be resolved long before the real event comes around.

The Germans have a deep well of knowhow and confidence born of tradition, which they can draw on in staging the World Cup. Apart from having hosted the finals once previously, West Germany also played host to the finals of the European Championship in 1988 and nine times staged the single-leg finals of the major club tournaments – the Champions League Cup, UEFA Cup and the now-defunct Cup-Winners' Cup.

In addition, the German-founded sportswear company adidas has been a

7. COLOGNE (KÖLN)

- Fixtures:
  11 June: ANG v POR 20.00 [D]
  17 June: CZE v GHA 17.00 [E]
  20 June: SWE v ENG 20.00 [B]
  23 June: TOG v FRA 20.00 [G]
  26 June: second-round match
- Tournament name: FIFA World Cup Stadium
- Bundesliga name: RheinEnergieStadion also Mungersdorferstadion
- Capacity: 46,120 (non-WC 50,997)
- Cost: €110million
- Car parking: 8,200
- Transport: car, bus, tram
- 1974 World Cup: not used

Club: FC Koln (Bundesliga)

The city (pop. one million): Romans established a small town in 50AD and the city takes its name from the Latin *Colonia*, meaning "colony". Its university, founded in 1388, is one of Europe's oldest and the magnificent twin-spired cathedral built on the banks of the Rhine is one of the continent's major gothic creations.

8. FRANKFURT AM MAIN

- Fixtures:
  10 June: ENG v PAR 14.00 [B]
  13 June: KOR v TOG 14.00 [G]
  17 June: POR v IRA 14.00 [D]
  21 June: HOL v ARG 20.00 [C]
  1 July: quarter-final
- Tournament name: Waldstadion
- Bundesliga name: Commerzbank-Arena, also Waldstadion
- Capacity: 43,324 (non-WC 48,132)
- Cost: €126million
- Car parking: 13,000
- Transport: car, tram, metro
- 1974 World Cup: five matches (including Opening Match: Brazil 0, Yugoslavia 0)

Club: Eintracht Frankfurt (Bundesliga)

The city (pop. 650,000): Situated in the state of Hesse, Frankfurt is Germany's financial capital as well as home of the German football federation (the Deutscher Fussball-Bund). Also founded by the Romans, Goethe's home city boasts Germany's main stock exchange, national bank headquarters and biggest airport.

9. KAISERSLAUTERN

- Fixtures:
  12 June: AUS v JAP 14.00 [F]
  17 June: ITA v USA 20.00 [E]
  20 June: PAR v TRI 20.00 [B]
  23 June: SAU v SPA 15.00 [H]
  26 June: second-round match
- Tournament name: Fritz-Walter-Stadion
- Bundesliga name: Fritz-Walter-Stadion
- Capacity: 41,513 (non-WC 48,500)
- Cost: €48.3million
- Car parking:
- Transport: rail, park-and-ride
- 1974 World Cup: not used

Club: FC Kaiserslautern (Bundesliga)

The city (pop. 100,000): Kaiserslautern, some 70 miles south-west of Frankfurt, is an industrial and university city whose sporting claim to fame was in providing the heart of West Germany's World Cup-winning team in 1954. The local stadium was named after the team's captain, Fritz Walter.

10. NUREMBERG (NÜRNBERG)

- Fixtures:
  11 June: MEX v IRA 17.00 [D]
  15 June: ENG v TRI 17.00 [B]
  18 June: JAP v CRO 14.00 [F]
  22 June: GHA v USA 15.00 [E]
  25 June: second-round match
- Tournament name: Franken-Stadion
- Bundesliga name: Franken-Stadion
- Capacity: 36,898 (non-WC 44,833)
- Cost: €56million
- Car parking: 15,000
- Transport: car, metro, rail, tram
- 1974 World Cup: not used

Club: FC Nurnberg (Bundesliga)

The city (pop. 490,000): Nuremberg, home to famous toy and Christmas fairs, was also the birthplace of the 13th-century poet Tannhauser and the setting for Richard Wagner's opera *The Mastersingers*. The heart of the medieval town, including some of the ancient walls and the 11th-century castle, has been restored.

11. STUTTGART

- Fixtures:
  13 June: FRA v SWI 17.00 [G]
  16 June: HOL v IVO 17.00 [C]
  19 June: SPA v TUN 20.00 [H]
  22 June: CRO v AUS 20.00 [F]
  25 June: second-round match
  8 July: third-place play-off
- Tournament name: Gottlieb-Daimler-Stadion
- Bundesliga name: Gottlieb-Daimler-Stadion
- Capacity: 47,757 (non-WC 56,800)
- Cost: €51.5million
- Car parking: 15,000
- Transport: car, bus, tram, rail
- 1974 World Cup: four matches

Club: VfB Stuttgart (Bundesliga)

The city (pop. 590,000): Stuttgart, on the Neckar river, is the state capital of Baden-Wurttemberg. It takes its name from a stud farm created in the 10th century – hence the horse on the coat of arms of the city. The Daimler-Benz factory, which was founded in 1890, remains the world's oldest car plant.

long-term commercial partner of both the German federation and FIFA.

One factor to surprise visitors is that the total stadia capacity for the World Cup of 573,297 is almost 110,000 below the capacity of the same grounds for German league matches.

The reasons are two-fold. Firstly, modern German stadia are designed deliberately with one specially designated section where fans can stand at Bundesliga matches. Temporary seating is then installed for matches in international competition as will be the case, of course, for the World Cup.

Secondly, a significant number of seats are not available for fans because of the enormous media presence. Other seats are 'lost' to the public because of additional security demands and also, in some cases, because of sight restrictions imposed by extra perimeter advertising.

Not that this detracts from the overall quality of the stadia, which are set to surpass those from the last World Cup finals held in Korea and Japan. As Beckenbauer says: "Thanks to the World Cup we now have the best stadia in the world and this is not only my opinion but that of visitors from around the world.

"We wanted stadia worthy of both the greatest players and the greatest event in world football."

12. MUNICH (MÜNCHEN)

- Fixtures:
  9 June: GER v COS 17.00 [A]
  14 June: TUN v SAU 17.00 [H]
  18 June: BRA v AUS 17.00 [F]
  21 June: IVO v SER 20.00 [C]
  24 June: second-round match
  5 July: semi-final
- Tournament name: FIFA World Cup Stadium
- Bundesliga name: Allianz-Arena
- Capacity: 59,416 (non-WC 66,016)
- Cost: €280million
- Car parking: 11,000
- Transport: car, metro
- 1974 World Cup: not built

Club: FC Bayern Munchen (Bundesliga), TSV 1860 Munchen (Second Bundesliga)

The city (pop. 1.3million): The historic home of the princely Wittelsbach dynasty is also the capital of the southern region of Bavaria. It produces cars, chemicals, cigarettes and, most famously, beer. On the dark side, Munich was also the birthplace of Adolf Hitler's Nazi movement in the 1920s.

HOW THEY QUALIFIED

THE LONG AND WINDING ROAD TO GERMANY

The statistics speak for themselves: 7,011 players from 194 countries produced 2,464 goals in 847 matches at an average of 2.91 per game in front of 18,657,843 fans during a 26-month marathon between September 2003 and November 2005. It all adds up to the planet's most ambitious intercontinental sports extravaganza.

Mission Control was at FIFA House, perched high on the Sonnenberg above Zurich in Switzerland, while the launch sites were the six regional confederations of Africa, Asia, Europe, Caribbean and North/Central America, Oceania and South America.

The outcome was the reduction of that near 200-strong field to 31 qualifiers to join hosts Germany in the finals.

Along the way history was made: this was the first time the holders had been denied direct entry into the finals. The decision, by FIFA's all-powerful executive before the 2002 finals, was greeted with bad grace by the national associations of both South America and Oceania.

Originally, FIFA had granted the Oceania winners direct entry, for the first time, to the 2006 finals. Previously Australia – usually – had to duel with lucky losers from Asia or South America and almost always lost. But FIFA's generosity to Oceania backfired. South America complained and part of the price of regaining half a place (!) was the loss of the holders' right to bypass qualifying.

Once again the CONMEBOL 10 opted for an all-in league of 18 matches apiece. Completing the marathon within the dates designated by the FIFA international calendar demanded kicking off a full two months before the official qualifying draw in Frankfurt.

Brazil thus launched their defence not in reunified Germany but in faraway Barranquilla, Colombia. Ronaldo and Juan Pablo Angel exchanged first-half goals before Kaka grabbed Brazil's winner on the hour. Fear of the unknown had been exorcised and the five-time winners duly progressed to top the group.

Argentina were edged on goal difference and Ecuador and Paraguay left a further six points adrift. Uruguay finished fifth and qualified for a repeat of their 2001 play-off against Australia.

On that occasion the 1930 and 1950 World Cup-winners lived up to their proud historical status by seeing off the Socceroos in the second leg in Montevideo. But this time that advantage had gone; the order of the ties was reversed. Australia lost 1–0 in the Estadio Centenario, reversed the score after extra time back in the Telstra stadium in Sydney and then triumphed 4–2 in the penalty shoot-out.

Middlesbrough keeper Mark Schwarzer was the hero; the only Socceroo to miss his spot-kick was national skipper and clubmate Mark Viduka. Uruguay ended up as the "dirtiest" team in qualifying with five red cards and 55 yellows.

Australia had played a mere seven matches until then, strolling with customary ease through the Oceania group stage. They won six of their games and drew the other, scored 30 goals, conceded four and picked up a top-notch manager along the way.

Guus Hiddink had steered Holland and then co-hosts South Korea to the semi-finals in 1998 and 2002 respectively. As one of the outstanding flying doctors of World Cup football he was perfectly suited to the split-time demands of Australia and Dutch club PSV Eindhoven.

Next time, the Australians will not have it so easy. They have quit Oceania for ultra-competitive Asia. The qualifying process will be far tougher. The 2002 qualifiers proved the point.

Iran, Japan, Saudi Arabia and South Korea battled through to Germany but none had it easy and all had to draw to

LEFT: The Socceroos jump for joy after beating mighty Uruguay 4–2 in a penalty shoot-out in the Telstra stadium, Sydney.

the full on previous qualifying experience. An envious bunch of almost equally powerful Asian nations fell just short.

Asia's qualifying competition involved 39 nations in a progression of mini-leagues, a system emulated and enhanced by the additional complication of two-leg play-offs in the Caribbean, Central and North America.

CONCACAF's politically astute president Jack Warner used the qualifying consistency of Mexico and the USA to persuade FIFA to increase its finals representation to three and a half. The Trinidadian was rewarded beyond his wildest dreams. Predictably Mexico and the US cruised through, followed by Costa Rica. The Mexicans were the qualifying top scorers with 67 goals.

Even better, CONCACAF not only saw their "lucky losers" beat Bahrain in the intercontinental play-offs . . . but the triumphant first-time finalists were Warner's "own" Trinidad & Tobago.

Bahrain protested to FIFA that a refereeing blunder had condemned them to undeserved defeat. The ploy worked, controversially, in their Asian play-off. A successful appeal against penalty-spot confusion created by Japanese referee Toshimitsu Yoshida had earned a replay victory over a furious Uzbekistan and their English manager, Bob Houghton.

This time, however, FIFA ruled the protest as lodged too late. Bahrain sulked, while Trinidad partied throughout a hastily declared national holiday.

Celebrations were also the order of the day in the five African nations whose qualifiers included no fewer than four newcomers. The giants of Cameroon, Egypt, Nigeria and South Africa all fell short, pipped by Angola, Ghana, Ivory Coast, Togo and the only 2002 qualifiers in Tunisia.

Failure was especially embarrassing for South Africa, four years ahead of their own hosting of the finals. Even more upset were Cameroon, because of the manner of their exit. They needed to beat Egypt at home to qualify. Germany beckoned when, at 1–1, they were awarded a stoppage-time penalty.

Chaos ensued as the players squabbled over who dared or dared not take it. In the end Inter full-back Pierre Wome grabbed the ball, set it on the penalty spot – and hit a post. He needed police protection all the way to the plane taking him back to Italy, while a furious mob trashed his home and forced his frightened family into hiding.

Europe, by contrast with Africa, raised only one newcomer nation: Ukraine. The former Soviet state, competing independently for only the third time, were the first European nation to book their ticket. They owed the achievement, above all, to the six goals of top-scoring Andriy Shevchenko.

Ukraine were followed by fellow group winners Holland, Portugal, France, Italy, England, Serbia & Montenegro and Croatia, plus the two designated runners-up with the best records – Poland and Sweden.

England stumbled their way to the top of Group Six despite an embarrassing 1–0 defeat by Northern Ireland on the run-in, their first upset in Belfast for 78 years.

England were not the only successful stumblers. The 1998 world champions France pulled themselves together only after recalling the likes of Zinedine Zidane, Lilian Thuram and Claude Makelele from international retirement. Even then they were the lowest-scoring of all the qualifying nations worldwide with a measly 14 goals.

Spain, maintaining their reputation for star-studded under-achievement, scrapped through courtesy of a play-off win over Slovakia.

Notable fallers included the European champions Greece. At least they took defeat comparatively graciously. This could not be said of Turkey. Having finished a best-ever third in 2002, they were denied a return to the finals – in Germany, where they would have been guaranteed huge émigré support – after losing both their play-off and their heads against Switzerland.

Ill will between both fans and players in both Berne and Istanbul prompted FIFA president Sepp Blatter to ponder the scrapping of national anthems. The idea was soon discarded. After all, what would the World Cup be without the national pride which has helped bring 32 nations so far?

RIGHT: Togo fans go crazy as their team qualifies for the World Cup finals for the first time. They are in Group D with France, Switzerland and S Korea.

BELOW: Frank Lampard hooks the ball into the Poland net to seal a 2–1 victory for England, which took them to the top of their qualifying group.

AFRICA (Five qualify)

STAGE ONE

Togo bt Equatorial Guinea 0-1, 2-0 (2-1 agg)
Zimbabwe bt Mauritania 3-0, 1-2 (4-2 agg)
Ghana bt Somalia 5-0, 2-0 (7-0 agg)
Zambia bt Seychelles 4-0, 1-1 (5-1 agg)
Angola bt Chad 1-3, 2-0 (away goals, 3-3 agg)
Mali bt Guinea-Bissau 2-1, 2-0 (4-1 agg)
Libya bt Sao Tome 1-0, 8-0 (9-0 agg)
Algeria v Niger 1-0, 6-0 (7-0 agg)
Kenya bt Tanzania 0-0, 3-0 (3-0 agg)
Burkina Faso walkover v Central African Rep
Benin bt Madagascar 1-1, 3-2 (4-3 agg)
Malawi bt Ethiopia 3-1, 0-0 (3-1 agg)
Guinea bt Mozambique 1-0, 4-3 (5-3 agg)
Botswana bt Lesotho 4-1, 0-0 (4-1 agg)
Congo bt Sierra Leone 1-0, 1-1 (2-1 agg)
Sudan bt Eritrea 3-0, 0-0 (3-0 agg)
Cape Verde Is bt Swaziland 1-1, 3-0 (4-1 agg)
Uganda bt Mauritius 3-0, 1-3 aet (4-3 agg)
Rwanda bt Namibia 3-0, 1-1 (4-1 agg)
Liberia bt Gambia 0-2, 3-0 (3-2 agg)
Gabon bt Burundi 0-0, 4-1 (4-1 agg)

STAGE TWO

Group 1

	P	W	D	L	F	A	Pts
TOGO	10	7	2	1	20	8	23
Senegal	10	6	3	1	21	8	21
Zambia	10	6	1	3	16	10	19
Congo	10	3	1	6	10	14	10
Mali	10	2	2	6	11	14	8
Liberia	10	1	1	8	8	27	4

Group 2

	P	W	D	L	F	A	Pts
GHANA	10	6	3	1	17	4	21
Congo DR	10	4	4	2	14	10	16
South Africa	10	5	1	4	12	14	16
Burkina Faso	10	4	1	5	14	13	13
Cape Verde Islands	10	3	1	6	8	15	10
Uganda	10	2	2	6	6	15	8

Group 3

	P	W	D	L	F	A	Pts
IVORY COAST	10	7	1	2	20	7	22
Cameroon	10	6	3	1	18	10	21
Egypt	10	5	2	3	26	15	17
Libya	10	3	3	4	8	10	12
Sudan	10	1	3	6	6	22	6
Benin	10	1	2	7	9	23	5

Group 4

	P	W	D	L	F	A	Pts
ANGOLA	10	6	3	1	12	6	21
Nigeria	10	6	3	1	21	7	21
Zimbabwe	10	4	3	3	13	14	15
Gabon	10	2	4	4	11	13	10
Algeria	10	1	5	4	8	15	8
Rwanda	10	1	2	7	6	16	5

Group 5

	P	W	D	L	F	A	Pts
TUNISIA	10	6	3	1	25	9	21
Morocco	10	5	5	0	17	7	20
Guinea	10	5	2	3	15	10	17
Kenya	10	3	1	6	8	10	10
Botswana	10	3	0	7	10	18	9
Malawi	10	1	3	6	12	26	6

Top scorer: 11 – Adebayor (Togo)

ASIA (Four qualify, one to play off)

STAGE ONE

Turkmenistan bt Afghanistan 11-0, 2-0 (13-0 agg)
Guam v Nepal, both withdrew
Chinese Tapei bt Macao 3-0, 3-1 (6-1 agg)
Tajikistan bt Bangladesh 2-0, 2-0 (4-0 agg)
Sri Lanka bt Laos 0-0, 3-0 (3-0 agg)
Kyrgyzstan bt Pakistan 2-0, 4-0 (6-0 agg)
Maldives bt Mongolia 1-0, 12-0 (13-0 agg)

STAGE TWO

Group 1

	P	W	D	L	F	A	Pts
Iran	6	5	0	1	22	4	15
Jordan	6	4	0	2	10	6	12
Qatar	6	3	0	3	16	8	9
Laos	6	0	0	6	3	33	0

Group 2

	P	W	D	L	F	A	Pts
Uzbekistan	6	5	1	0	16	3	16
Iraq	6	3	2	1	17	7	11
Palestine	6	2	1	3	11	11	7
Chinese Taipei	6	0	0	6	3	26	0

Group 3

	P	W	D	L	F	A	Pts
Japan	6	6	0	0	16	1	18
Oman	6	3	1	2	14	3	10
India	6	1	1	4	18	18	4
Singapore	6	1	0	5	3	13	3

Group 4

	P	W	D	L	F	A	Pts
Kuwait	6	5	0	1	15	2	15
China	6	5	0	1	14	1	15
Hong Kong	6	2	0	4	5	15	6
Malaysia	6	0	0	6	2	18	0

Group 5

	P	W	D	L	F	A	Pts
North Korea	6	3	2	1	11	5	11
UAE	6	3	1	2	6	6	10
Thailand	6	2	1	3	9	10	7
Yemen	6	1	2	3	6	11	5

Group 6

	P	W	D	L	F	A	Pts
Bahrain	6	4	2	0	15	4	14
Syria	6	2	2	2	7	7	8
Tajikistan	6	2	1	3	5	9	7
Kyrgyzstan	6	1	1	4	5	12	4

Group 7

	P	W	D	L	F	A	Pts
South Korea	6	4	2	0	9	2	14
Lebanon	6	3	2	1	11	5	11
Vietnam	6	1	1	4	5	9	4
Maldives	6	1	1	4	5	14	4

Group 8

	P	W	D	L	F	A	Pts
Saudi Arabia	6	6	0	0	14	1	18
Turkmenistan	6	2	1	3	8	10	7
Indonesia	6	2	1	3	8	12	7
Sri Lanka	6	0	2	4	4	11	2

STAGE THREE

Group A

	P	W	D	L	F	A	Pts
SAUDI ARABIA	6	4	2	0	10	1	14
SOUTH KOREA	6	3	1	2	9	5	10
Uzbekistan	6	1	2	3	7	11	5
Kuwait	6	1	1	4	4	13	4

Group B

	P	W	D	L	F	A	Pts
JAPAN	6	5	0	1	9	4	15
IRAN	6	4	1	1	7	3	13
Bahrain	6	1	1	4	4	7	4
North Korea	6	1	0	5	5	11	3

PLAY-OFF

Bahrain bt Uzbekistan 1-1, 0-0 (away goal, 1-1 agg)
Bahrain qual for intercontinental play-off
Top scorer: 9 - Ali Daei (Iran)

EUROPE (13 qualify - eight group winners plus two runners-up and three via play-offs)

Group 1

	P	W	D	L	F	A	Pts
HOLLAND	12	10	2	0	27	3	32
Czech Republic	12	9	0	3	35	12	27
Romania	12	8	1	3	20	10	25
Finland	12	5	1	6	21	19	16
Macedonia	12	2	3	7	11	24	9
Armenia	12	2	1	9	9	25	7
Andorra	12	1	2	9	4	34	5

Group 2

	P	W	D	L	F	A	Pts
UKRAINE	12	7	4	1	18	7	25
Turkey	12	6	5	1	23	9	23
Denmark	12	6	4	2	24	12	22
Greece	12	6	3	3	15	9	21
Albania	12	4	1	7	11	20	13
Georgia	12	2	4	6	14	25	10
Kazakhstan	12	0	1	11	6	29	1

Group 3

	P	W	D	L	F	A	Pts
PORTUGAL	12	9	3	0	35	5	30
Slovakia	12	6	5	1	24	8	23
Russia	12	6	5	1	23	12	23
Estonia	12	5	2	5	16	17	17
Latvia	12	4	3	5	18	21	15
Liechtenstein	12	2	2	8	13	23	8
Luxembourg	12	0	0	12	5	48	0

Group 4

	P	W	D	L	F	A	Pts
FRANCE	10	5	5	0	14	2	20
Switzerland	10	4	6	0	18	7	18
Israel	10	4	6	0	15	10	18
Rep Ireland	10	4	5	1	12	5	17
Cyprus	10	1	1	8	8	20	4
Faroe Islands	10	0	1	9	4	27	1

Group 5

	P	W	D	L	F	A	Pts
ITALY	10	7	2	1	17	8	23
Norway	10	5	3	2	12	7	18
Scotland	10	3	4	3	9	7	13
Slovenia	10	3	3	4	10	13	12
Belarus	10	2	4	4	12	14	10
Moldova	10	1	2	5	5	16	5

Group 6

	P	W	D	L	F	A	Pts
ENGLAND	10	8	1	1	17	5	25
POLAND	10	8	0	2	27	9	24
Austria	10	4	3	3	15	12	15
N Ireland	10	2	3	5	10	18	9
Wales	10	2	2	6	10	15	8
Azerbaijan	10	0	3	7	1	21	3

Group 7

	P	W	D	L	F	A	Pts
SERBIA	10	6	4	0	16	1	22
Spain	10	5	5	0	19	3	20
Bosnia	10	4	4	2	12	9	16
Belgium	10	3	3	4	16	11	12
Lithuania	10	2	4	4	8	9	10
San Marino	10	0	0	10	2	40	0

Group 8

	P	W	D	L	F	A	Pts
CROATIA	10	7	3	0	21	5	24
SWEDEN	10	8	0	2	30	4	24
Bulgaria	10	4	3	3	17	17	15
Hungary	10	4	2	4	13	14	14
Iceland	10	1	1	8	14	27	4
Malta	10	0	3	7	4	32	3

PLAY-OFFS

Czech Republic bt Norway 1-0, 1-0 (2-0 agg)
Spain bt Slovakia 5-1, 1-1 (6-2 agg)
Switzerland bt Turkey 2-0, 2-4 (away goals, 4-4 agg)

Top scorer: 11 – Pauleta (Portugal)

NORTH & CENTRAL AMERICA & CARRIBEAN

(Three qualify, one to play off)

STAGE ONE

Group 1

United States bt Grenada 3-0, 3-2 (6-2 agg)

Group 2

Bermuda bt Montserrat 13-0, 7-0 (20-0 agg)
El Salvador bt Bermuda 2-1, 2-2 (4-3 agg)

Group 3

Haiti bt Turks & Caicos 5-0, 2-0 (7-0 agg)
Jamaica bt Haiti 1-1, 3-0 (4-1 agg)

Group 4

St Lucia bt British Virgin Is 1-0, 9-0 (10-0 agg)
Panama bt St Lucia 4-0, 3-0 (7-0 agg)

Group 5

Cuba bt Cayman Is 2-1, 3-0 (5-1)
Costa Rica bt Cuba 2-2, 1-1 (away goals, 3-3 agg)

Group 6

Surinam bt Aruba 2-1, 8-1 (10-2)
Guatemala bt Surinam 1-1, 3-1 (4-2 agg)

Group 7

Netherlands Antilles bt Antigua & Barbuda 0-2, 3-0 (3-2 agg)
Honduras bt Netherlands Antilles 2-1, 4-0 (6-1 agg)

Group 8

Canada bt Belize 4-0, 4-0 (8-0 agg)

Group 9

Dominica bt Bahamas 1-1, 3-1 (4-2 agg)
Mexico bt Domenica 10-0 (single match)

Group 10

St Kitts & Nevis bt US Virgin Is 4-0, 7-0 (11-0 agg)
St Kitts & Nevis bt Barbados 2-0, 3-2 (5-2 agg)

Group 11

Dominican Republic bt Anguilla 0-0, 6-0 (6-0 agg)
Trinidad & Tobago bt Dominican Republic 2-0, 4-0 (6-0 agg)

Group 12

St Vincent & Grenadines bt Nicaragua 2-2, 4-1 (6-3 on agg)

STAGE TWO

Group 1

	P	W	D	L	F	A	Pts
United States	6	3	3	0	13	3	12
Panama	6	2	2	2	8	11	8
Jamaica	6	1	4	1	7	5	7
El Salvador	6	1	1	4	2	11	4

Group 2

	P	W	D	L	F	A	Pts
Costa Rica	6	3	1	2	12	8	10
Guatemala	6	3	1	2	7	9	10
Honduras	6	1	4	1	9	7	7
Canada	6	1	2	3	4	8	5

Group 3

	P	W	D	L	F	A	Pts
Mexico	6	6	0	0	27	1	18
Trinidad	6	4	0	2	12	9	12
St Vincent	6	2	0	4	5	12	6
St Kitts	6	0	0	6	2	24	0

STAGE THREE

League Round

	P	W	D	L	F	A	Pts
UNITED STATES	10	7	1	2	16	6	22
MEXICO	10	7	1	2	22	9	22
COSTA RICA	10	5	1	4	15	14	16
Trinidad	10	4	1	5	10	15	13
Guatemala	10	3	2	5	16	18	11
Panama	10	0	2	8	4	21	2

**Trinidad & Tobago qual for intercontinental play-off

Top scorer: 14 – Borgetti (Mexico)

OCEANIA (One to play off)

STAGE ONE

Group 1

	P	W	D	L	F	A	Pts
Solomon Is.	4	3	1	0	14	1	10
Tahiti	4	2	2	0	5	1	8
New Caledonia	4	2	1	1	16	2	7
Tonga	4	1	0	3	2	17	3
Cook Is.	4	0	0	4	1	17	0

Group 2

	P	W	D	L	F	A	Pts
Vanuatu	4	3	1	0	16	2	10
Fiji	4	3	0	1	19	5	9
Papua N.G.	4	2	1	1	17	6	7
Samoa	4	1	0	3	5	11	3
American Samoa	4	0	0	4	1	34	0

STAGE TWO

League Round

	P	W	D	L	F	A	Pts
Australia	5	4	1	0	21	3	13
Solomon Is.	5	3	1	1	9	6	10
New Zealand	5	3	0	2	17	5	9
Fiji	5	1	1	3	3	10	4
Tahiti	5	1	1	3	2	24	4
Vanuatu	5	1	0	4	5	9	3

STAGE THREE

Australia bt Solomon Islands 7-0, 2-1 (9-1 agg)
Australia qual for intercontinental play-off
Top scorer(s): 7 – Cahill (Australia), Toma (Fiji)

SOUTH AMERICA (Four qualify, one to play off)

League Round

	P	W	D	L	F	A	Pts
BRAZIL	18	9	7	2	35	17	34
ARGENTINA	18	10	4	4	29	17	34
ECUADOR	18	8	4	6	23	19	28
PARAGUAY	18	8	4	6	23	23	28
Uruguay	18	6	7	5	23	28	25
Colombia	18	6	6	6	24	16	24
Chile	18	5	7	6	22	22	22
Venezuela	18	5	3	10	20	28	18
Peru	18	4	6	8	20	28	18
Bolivia	18	4	2	12	20	37	14

Top scorer: 10 – Ronaldo (Brazil)

INTERCONTINENTAL PLAY-OFFS

CONCACAF v Asia

Trinidad & Tobago bt Bahrain 1-1, 1-0 (2-1 agg)

Oceania v South America

Australia bt Uruguay 1-0, 0-1 aet (4-2 pens, 1-1 agg)

BELOW: Angola's striker Fabrice Akwa is swamped by team-mates after he scored the only goal against Rwanda which took them to the finals.

BBB RAMA
SEMBLJCI
MA LA
SUBO TICA
ČITLUČANI
Ožujsko Ožujsko Ožujsko

THE TEAMS

ALL CREATURES GREAT AND SMALL

World Cup football is about not only style but styles. It's a unique mixture of the best the international game has to offer. Many of the outstanding memories down the years have been offered up not only by the traditional grandees of the game but by the minnows.

North Korea appeared only once at the finals but will never be forgotten for their exploits in 1966 when they beat Italy 1–0. Iran, Costa Rica and Algeria have written remarkable pages in the competition's history, while Cameroon enforced a new respect for African football in 1990 by first beating holders Argentina then reaching the quarter-finals before finally succumbing to England in extra time.

The 32 nations attending the 2006 finals can be grouped into even more fascinating "pots" than the glass vases on stage at the draw in Leipzig.

Talk of the World Cup inspires countless images of the unmatchable touch and technique of Brazil for whom Robinho, Ronaldo and Ronaldinho – who scooped every major individual international award in 2005 – represent a continuation of the tradition established by superstars from Leonidas in 1938 to Pele some 20 years later.

Southern neighbours Argentina add a steely element to the Latin American challenge with the marvellous creative talents of playmaker Juan Roman Riquelme and striker Hernan Crespo balanced by the defensive rigour of Walter Samuel and midfield drive of Juan Sorin.

Uruguay's failure to defeat Australia in the climactic qualifying play-off left Ecuador and Paraguay to complete the South American challenge, while Mexico and Costa Rica add their own stylistic and tactical variations to the Latin American mix. But Mexico and Costa Rica represent only half of the North/Central American and Caribbean challenge.

The United States have long since cast away the image of football outsiders and were unlucky not to feature among the top seeds since they stood eighth in the world rankings at the time of the draw. They are competing in their fifth successive finals and reached the quarter-finals four years ago.

Completing the four-strong CONCACAF group are newcomers Trinidad & Tobago who leaned on the experience of veteran Premiership forward Dwight Yorke to battle exuberantly through a 20-match series, ending in a dramatic intercontinental play-off victory over Bahrain. Dennis Lawrence, from Wrexham in what is effectively the English fourth division, scored the goal which booked their ticket to Germany.

Bahrain's failure left sprawling Asia with four finalists headed by 2002 co-hosts Japan and South Korea plus Saudi Arabia and Iran. Japan intend at least to match their second-round finish back then though it would be a major surprise if the Koreans, lacking their fanatical home support, stormed to the semi-finals again.

The largest block of debutants arises out of Africa. Regular recent finalists such as Cameroon, Nigeria and South Africa were left kicking themselves rather than the official adidas "teamgeist" footballs after falling under the eager challenge of Angola, Ghana, Ivory Coast and Togo. Only Tunisia, completing Africa's five-strong entry, have previously basked in the finals limelight – and they have never progressed beyond round one.

Australia can say the same. But then, they have appeared only once before in the finals – coincidentally in then West Germany 32 years ago. Then they lost 3–0 to their hosts and went home after the first round. But that was a different Australia: all their players, for example, were with Australian clubs. Evidence of the great leap forward is that almost all today's heroes feature in the top divisions of western Europe.

That was one reason why many of the coaches of the 14 European finalists hoped to avoid the Socceroos in the draw: their European know-how and wise guidance of Dutch master coach Guus Hiddink marked them out as dangerous dark horses in the early stages. Coping is the challenge for Brazil, Croatia and Japan.

All of Europe's giants join the party. Some – such as Croatia, England, France, Holland, Italy, Portugal, Poland and Sweden – eased through more easily than the likes of Spain, the Czech Republic and Switzerland who all needed the fallback option offered by the play-off route.

The only European newcomers are Ukraine, spearheaded by Andriy Shevchenko, though Serbia & Montenegro compete for the first time in this guise as successors to the footballing mantle of the former Yugoslavia.

Latin American technique, African excitement, Caribbean exuberance and European commitment add up to a perfect recipe for the football feast ahead.

LEFT: Calm before the storm: Croatia and Sweden players shake hands before their qualifying match.

BELOW: Match officials lead out the teams as England and Poland prepare for battle at Old Trafford.

GERMANY

THE PRESSURE IS ON

Hosts Germany will be expected to win by many fans. But coach Jurgen Klinsmann is having to build a new team. Their most dangerous opponents could be the weight of history and the pressure of expectation that being the host nation brings.

Jurgen Klinsmann has brought about a management revolution in his attempt to emulate Franz Beckenbauer and win the World Cup with Germany as both player and then manager.

The Germans have an impressive World Cup pedigree. They are one of only two European nations – with Italy – to have won the Cup three times; they have also finished runners-up on three occasions and have been semi-finalists in three tournaments.

But the last win was back in 1990 when Klinsmann scored three of the then West Germany's 14 goals in the run to their 1–0 final victory over Argentina in Rome. Since then the Germans have proved a consistent disappointment to their own fans who fear that the production line of outstanding players has ground to a standstill.

Klinsmann does not accept that pessimistic view. On being appointed after Germany crashed out in the first round of Euro 2004, he said: "We still have lots of bright young players, but they lack confidence and the national team structures have let them down."

The baker's son from Gottingen near Stuttgart knows all about structures. After retiring in 1996 he and his American wife left Europe to set up home on the Pacific coast in southern California. Klinsmann occupied himself by going back to college to study management and administration.

When the German federation turned to him in desperation to succeed Rudi Voller – after being turned down by Ottmar Hitzfeld – they had not bargained on Klinsmann's abiding self-confidence.

He demanded a complete separation of the national team organization from the rest of the DFB and the right to appoint his own staff in place of virtually all Voller's backroom team.

German football is proud of its heritage and the achievements of past greats such as Fritz Szepan and Ernst Kuzorra in the 1930s, the Walter brothers and Helmut Rahn in the 1950s, Uwe Seeler in the 1960s and Beckenbauer, Gerd Muller and Sepp Maier and their Bayern Munich successors such as Karl-Heinz Rummenigge in the 1970s and 1980s.

"But we cannot live in the past," says Klinsmann. "Just because we used to do everything one way does not mean we must live in the past. You do not win today's matches with yesterday's players and systems."

The manner in which Klinsmann set about rebuilding the team in the wake of the Euro 2004 debacle divided opinion throughout Germany. He dropped many of the senior players, albeit after assuring them that they would still be considered for the World Cup "after we have seen what the youngsters can do".

Most controversially, he refused to decide on his first-choice goalkeeper

LEFT: Oliver Kahn is one of the most aggressive goalkeepers football has seen. "The Boss of the Box", as he is known, is most unhappy at having to share the German gloves with Jens Lehmann.

WORLD CUP RECORD

1930 did not enter	1974 champions
1934 third place	1978 2nd round
1938 1st round	1982 runners-up
1950 did not enter	1986 runners-up
1954 champions	1990 champions
1958 fourth place	1994 quarter-finals
1962 quarter-finals	1998 quarter-finals
1966 runners-up	2002 runners-up
1970 third place	

STAR PERFORMERS

Oliver Kahn
↗ Goalkeeper ↗ Bayern Munich
↗ Born: June 15, 1969

Cristoph Metzelder
↗ Central defender ↗ Borussia Dortmund
↗ Born: November 5, 1980

Bernd Schneider
↗ Midfielder ↗ Bayer Leverkusen
↗ Born: November 17, 1973

Bastian Schweinsteiger
↗ Forward ↗ Bayern Munich
↗ Born: August 1, 1984

Kevin Kuranyi
↗ Striker ↗ Schalke ↗ Born: March 2, 1982

THE ROAD TO THE FINALS

Qualified direct as hosts

and played Bayern Munich's Oliver Kahn and Arsenal's Jens Lehmann in alternate games. That infuriated the Bayern contingent and led directly to the sacking of Maier as Germany's goalkeeper coach.

But Klinsmann would not be deflected from his path, saying: "I want competition in every position. No-one has an automatic right to a place in the team."

The only player who comes anywhere close to that assumption is Michael Ballack.

Bayern Munich's midfield leader was Germany's outstanding outfield player at the 2002 finals in South Korea and should be at the peak of his powers this time around.

Supporting him will be improving young defenders such as centre-backs Robert Huth and Christoph Metzelder, full-back Philipp Lahm, experienced midfielders such as Bernd Schneider and Torsten Frings plus the bright new heroes of a younger generation up front in Bastian Schweinsteiger, Lukas Podolski and Kevin Kuranyi from Schalke.

Schweinsteiger, an electric-heeled winger, proved one of the bright young revelations of the 2004 European Championship finals in Portugal and underlined his star status with subsequent performances the following year when Germany reached the semi-finals of the Confederations Cup on home soil.

Kuranyi is an exciting, cosmopolitan mixture. Born in Brazil to a German father and Panamanian mother, Kuranyi made his name with Stuttgart then moved to Schalke to gain a Champions League education in the season leading up to the World Cup.

How Klinsmann's new team will cope with the host nation pressures is an unknown factor.

Klinsmann knows that "it's great to have your own fans in the stadia but the downside is that they can also get impatient very quickly".

This is the reason he added a psychologist to his management staff, to help ensure his players were ready both physically and mentally for the challenge ahead.

Whatever the outcome of Germany's World Cup, they will not lack the most thorough preparation.

COACH

Jurgen Klinsmann

↗ Born: July 30, 1964

Klinsmann was a World Cup-winning striker for West Germany in Italy in 1990. After a club career with Stuttgart, Internazionale (Italy), Monaco (France), Tottenham (England, twice) and Bayern Munich, he retired from the game to family life in California. Recalled for his first managerial post, with Germany, in the summer of 2004.

STAR PLAYER

Michael Ballack

↗ Midfielder ↗ Bayern Munich

↗ Born: September 26, 1976

Born and brought up in the former East Germany, Ballack began with Chemnitz but made his Bundesliga breakthrough with Kaiserslautern. He gained Under-21 recognition in the Lauterers' surprise league title-winning campaign before transferring to Bayer Leverkusen with whom he was a Champions League runner-up in 2002. Ballack switched that summer to Bayern Munich after inspiring Germany to reach the World Cup final. Unfortunately he missed the duel with Brazil through suspension after a second yellow card in the semi-final win over South Korea. Ballack, twice German Footballer of the Year, was appointed national captain in autumn 2004.

POLAND

THE EXILES ELEVEN

Powerful Poland are heading back onto the big stage after having twice finished third at the World Cup finals. This time, however, it's their foreign-based players on whom they will be relying to make all the difference.

Pawel Janas played his part in one of Poland's great achievements – finishing third in the 1982 World Cup finals. Now the former Legia Warsaw defender bids to emulate such achievements as Poland's coach.

Janas was ever-present in defence when the Poles reached the last four in Spain. But without him they reached only the second round in Mexico four years later and did not qualify for the finals again until 2002, in Japan and South Korea. Then they finished bottom of Group D behind Portugal, the United States and group winners South Korea.

That team was a pale shadow of the great side between 1972 and 1982. Poland served notice of their rise by winning Olympic football gold in 1972, then eliminating England to reach the 1974 World Cup finals.

Their heroes in West Germany included acrobatic goalkeeper Jan Tomaszweski, central defenders Jerzy Gorgon and Wladyslaw Zmuda, playmaker Kazimierz Deyna and the flying wingers Grzegorz Lato and Robert Gadocha.

The Poles beat Argentina, Haiti and Italy in the first round then edged both Sweden and Yugoslavia in the second phase to set up what was effectively a semi-final against West Germany in Frankfurt. Tomaszewski saved an Uli Hoeness penalty but Gerd Muller scored the only goal. The Poles duly finished third by beating Brazil 1–0 in the play-off while Lato was crowned tournament top scorer with seven goals.

In 1978, in Argentina, Poland topped their first-phase group, then were duly eliminated after losing to Argentina and Brazil.

But a major difference exists between Poland's golden decade and the side Janas coaches. In 1974 and 1978, all the players came from Polish clubs. In 1982, the 32-year-old Lato, then with the Belgian side Lokeren, was the only player based outside Poland.

That era ended with reforms forced on the communist government by the Solidarity labour movement. At last Poland's stars were freed to move abroad in their 20s, at the peak of their careers. Thus Janas joined French club Auxerre soon after the finals.

So the balance has changed. Janas's first squad for the qualifiers did not include one home-based player. As he says: "It's a problem sometimes getting the players together. We don't have much time. We can work only on our formation, tactics and set-pieces."

Liverpool goalkeeper Jerzy Dudek sees advantages though. He says: "The experience gained by the players who have gone abroad in the last

WORLD CUP RECORD

1930 did not enter	1974 third place
1934 did not qualify	1978 2nd round
1938 1st round	1982 third place
1950 did not enter	1986 2nd round
1954 did not enter	1990 did not qualify
1958 did not qualify	1994 did not qualify
1962 did not qualify	1998 did not qualify
1966 did not qualify	2002 1st round
1970 did not qualify	

STAR PERFORMERS

Michal Zewlakov
↗ Full-back ↗ Anderlecht
↗ Born: April 22, 1976

Jacek Bak
↗ Central defender ↗ Al-Rayyan
↗ Born: March 24, 1973

Jacek Krzynowek
↗ Midfielder ↗ Bayer Leverkusen
↗ Born: May 15, 1976

Maciej Zurawski
↗ Forward ↗ Celtic
↗ Born: September 12, 1976

Grzegorz Rasiak
↗ Centre-forward ↗ Tottenham Hotspur
↗ Born: January 12, 1979

LEFT: Veteran defender Tomasz Hajto, who specializes in long throw-ins.

THE ROAD TO THE FINALS

W 3-0	away v Northern Ireland (Zurawski, Wlodarczyk, Krzynowek)
L 1-2	home v England (Zurawski)
W 3-1	away v Austria (Kaluzny, Krzynowek, Frankowski)
W 3-2	away v Wales (Frankowski, Zurawski, Krzynowek)
W 8-0	home v Azerbaijan (Frankowski 3, Hajiev og, Kosowski, Krzynowek, Saganowski 2)
W 1-0	home v Northern Ireland (Zurawski)
W 3-0	away v Azerbaijan (Frankowski, Klos, Zurawski)
W 3-2	home v Austria (Smolarek, Kusowski, Zurawski)
W 1-0	home v Wales (Zurawski)
L 1-2	away v England (Frankowski)

STAR PLAYER

Jerzy Dudek

↗ Goalkeeper ↗ Liverpool

↗ Born: March 23, 1973

Dudek established a reputation as one of Europe's finest goalkeepers during a five-year spell with Feyenoord in Holland. His agility and sharp reflexes made him as much a favourite in Rotterdam as he had been earlier back home with GKS Tychy. Liverpool signed him in 2001 for £4.8million, but it took Dudek time to adjust to the pace and aggression of the Premiership. Ironically it was only when his place at Anfield came under serious threat that he hit his heroic best. In the 2005 Champions League Final victory over Milan, he saved brilliantly from Andriy Shevchenko in the last minutes of extra-time and then stopped the Ukrainian's decisive last penalty.

COACH

Pawel Janas

↗ Born: March 4, 1953

Janas, a former international central defender, played 50 times for Poland and enjoyed a successful career as a stalwart of Pabianice, Widzew Lodz, Legia Warsaw and French club Auxerre before returning home to take up coaching. Took over as national boss from ex-team-mate Zibi Boniek in the autumn of 2002 after three years as boss of the Under-21s.

year or two has definitely helped the national side."

Janas, who usually employs a 4-4-2 formation, has largely picked his forwards from among Celtic striker Maciej Zurawski, Tottenham's Gregorz Rasiak and seven-goal joint top scorer Tomasz Frankowski of Spanish second division club Eiche CF. The coach dropped his injury-prone striker Emmanuel Olisadebe for the concluding qualifier against England.

Borussia Dortmund's Ebi Smolarek – son of 1982 hero Wlodzimierz – and Leverkusen's Jacek Krynowek can supply width in midfield, Trabzonspor's Miroslav Szymkowiak is a skilled playmaker while Arek Radomski of FK Austria Vienna prefers the anchor role.

Poland have vast experience in defence in the shape of skipper Jacek Bak, Tomasz Klos, now back home with Wisla Krakow, Den Haag veteran Tomasz Rzasa and Anderlecht's Michal Zewlakow.

Antoni Piechniczek, coach of the 1982 side, summed up Janas's team by saying: "This present generation owe their place in the finals not to any one individual but to their overall consistency."

Dudek says: "The heroes of 1974 will never be forgotten by our fans. But we don't want to compete with past glories. We want to make our own. We've built up a momentum and that's created a tremendous spirit in the squad."

Poland's preparations for the 2006 qualifiers were thrown into chaos when they crashed 5–1 to Denmark in a warm-up friendly. Janas considered resignation. He said: "We have no time for experiments any more."

Poland opened with a 3–0 win over Northern Ireland in Belfast. A 2–1 home defeat by England was a setback. But the Poles' confidence soared with two away wins in four days, in October 2004.

Radek Kaluzny, Krzynowek and Frankowski netted in a 3–1 victory over Austria in Vienna, a game Poland finished with 10 men after Radomski was sent off. Then they came from behind to beat Wales 3–2 in Cardiff courtesy of strikes from Frankowski, the goal-hungry Maciej Zurawski and Krzynowek.

Two demolitions of Azerbaijan and home wins over Northern Ireland, Austria and Wales ensured Poland's qualification – as one of the best runners-up – after their 2–1 defeat by England at Old Trafford.

Now they must try to live up to their country's World Cup tradition.

COSTA RICA

BOUNCEBACKABILITY

Paulo Wanchope and his Ticos left it late to snatch their tickets for the finals, but now their ambition is to spring the sort of surprise which first brought them to the world's astonished attention back in Italy in 1990.

Think Costa Rica and the World Cup and one match inevitably springs to mind – the 1–0 win masterminded by coach Bora Milutinovic over Scotland at Italia 90, which still ranks as one of the tournament's great upsets.

It was Costa Rica's first appearance in the finals and, although the result had every self-respecting Scotsman crying into his beer, it is often forgotten that Sweden also capitulated in the group stage that year to the tiny Central American country who qualified for the second round where they were eventually roundly trounced by Czechoslovakia.

Not until the last World Cup in Japan and Korea did Costa Rica return to the big stage where they put on another brave performance. They beat China and drew with eventual semi-finalists Turkey, before bowing out in the group stage on goal difference.

Now they are back once more, again carrying the tag of rank outsiders after finishing a distant six points behind Mexico and United States in the CONCACAF zone. It was still enough to clinch third spot – despite three changes of coach – and a ticket to Germany.

At one point they wobbled badly during qualifying, losing four of their 10 final round matches. However, the Ticos have a habit of hitting the ground running and raising their game during the finals themselves and their attacking verve should not be under-estimated – a quality illustrated in the 5–2 defeat by Brazil in 2002 which sealed Costa Rica's fate but whose margin flattered the eventual champions.

Qualification for Germany was clinched with a 3–0 win over the United States, albeit against an experimental side since the Americans had already qualified. This was not the first time Costa Rica had been given a helping hand by their American colleagues. Back in 1989, a 0–0 draw between the US and Guatemala handed Costa Rica their first ever berth in the finals, while a 2–0 win over the US in September 2001 ensured qualification for Korea and Japan. Now all their hopes for springing further upsets on the world stage rest with their record international marksman, Paulo Wanchope.

WORLD CUP RECORD

1930-54 did not enter	1982 did not qualify
1958 did not qualify	1986 did not qualify
1962 did not qualify	1990 2nd round
1966 did not qualify	1994 did not qualify
1970 did not qualify	1998 did not qualify
1974 did not qualify	2002 1st round
1978 did not qualify	

STAR PLAYER

Paulo Wanchope
↗ Striker ↗ Al Garafah
↗ Born: July 31, 1976

Wanchope hopes to end his international career in style after wrapping up qualifying with a Costa Rica record of 43 goals in 67 games. Clubs have included England's Derby, West Ham and Manchester City plus Spain's Malaga.

STAR PERFORMERS

Alvaro Mesen
↗ Goalkeeper ↗ CS Herediano
↗ Born: December 24, 1972

Luis Antonio Marin
↗ Defender ↗ LD Alajuelense
↗ Born: August 10, 1974

Harold Wallace
↗ Defender ↗ LD Alajuelense
↗ Born: September 7, 1975

Walter Centeno
↗ Midfielder ↗ Deportivo Saprissa
↗ Born: October 6, 1974

Ronald Gomez
↗ Striker ↗ Deportivo Saprissa
↗ Born: January 24, 1975

COACH

Alexandre Guimaraes
↗ Born: November 7, 1959
↗ Appointed April 2005
↗ Previous Deportivo Saprissa, CSD Comunicaciones (Guatemala), Costa Rica, Irapuato (Mexico), Dorados de Sinaloa (Mexico)

THE ROAD TO THE FINALS

1st round	
D 2-2	away v Cuba (Sequeira, Saborio)
D 1-1	home v Cuba (Gomez)
Costa Rica on away goals, 3-3 agg	
2nd round	
L 2-5	home v Honduras (Herron 2)
L 1-2	away v Guatemala (Solis)
W 1-0	home v Canada (Wanchope)
W 5-0	home v Guatemala (Wanchope 3, Hernandez, Fonseca)
W 3-1	away v Canada (Wanchope, Sunsing, Hernandez)
D 0-0	away v Honduras
L 1-2	home v Mexico (Wanchope)
W 2-1	home v Panama (Wilson, Myre)
D 0-0	away v Trinidad and Tobago
L 0-3	away v United States
W 3-2	home v Guatemala (Hernandez, Gomez, Wanchope)
L 0-2	away v Mexico
W 3-1	away v Panama (Saborio, Centeno, Gomez)
W 2-0	home v Trinidad and Tobago (Saborio, Centeno)
W 3-0	home v United States (Wanchope, Hernandez 2)
L 1-3	away v Guatemala (Myre)

ECUADOR

ON A HIGH

Ecuador made history four years ago on their World Cup debut. But the team who beat Brazil and Argentina on the way to the finals this time around must keep their feet on the ground if they want to make further progress.

Having enjoyed their first taste four years ago of the unique atmosphere to be enjoyed at the World Cup finals, Ecuador are back for more in Germany. This time they arrive with a Colombian coach whom they had to send for in an emergency.

Make no mistake, however, about Luis Suarez's loyalty or determination to achieve "something special" rather than be eliminated at the group stage as Ecuador were in Korea and Japan.

The burning question is, how will Ecuador fare on foreign soil this time around? Of the 28 points which earned them a place in the finals, 23 were gained at home in Quito, not least because of the altitude that hampered their rivals.

Even Brazil and Argentina were brought to their knees at the Atahualpa stadium and Suarez's challenge is to ensure he can keep his players' feet on the ground once they are away from their home fortress. "There's no denying that playing at altitude was a determining factor," he said. "But we are where we are because we have a good team."

The evidence stacks up. Third place behind the two South American superpowers of Brazil and Argentina speaks for itself. Qualification was clinched with one match day left, despite a disastrous Copa America in 2004 which led to a managerial clear-out and a partial overhaul of the squad.

Christian Lara is the new kid on the block. El Nacional's attacking midfielder put in a stunning display against Argentina when he was called up to replace the injured 2002 hero Edison Mendez.

Already compared to Brazil's Robinho, the diminutive Lara is just one of several players who make Ecuador dangerous floaters. Others include Mendez, Ulises De la Cruz and Agustin Delgado, all members of the so-called Golden Generation who want to bow out in glory.

Delgado says: "We now have more important and ambitious young players who, just like us, came up through the system. They are the future of our football which, in recent years, has come on in leaps and bounds. We are capable of achieving great things."

That depends which Ecuador turn up: the team who beat Argentina and Brazil in qualifying or the one comprehensively dismantled by minnows Venezuela.

WORLD CUP RECORD

1930-58 did not enter	1982 did not qualify
1962 did not qualify	1986 did not qualify
1966 did not qualify	1990 did not qualify
1970 did not qualify	1994 did not qualify
1974 did not qualify	1998 did not qualify
1978 did not qualify	2002 1st round

STAR PERFORMERS

Ulises De la Cruz
↗ Full-back ↗ Aston Villa
↗ Born: February 8, 1974

Ivan Hurtado
↗ Defender ↗ Pachuca
↗ Born: August 16, 1974

Edison Mendez
↗ Midfielder ↗ Liga Deportiva Universitaria
↗ Born: March 16, 1979

Christian Rolando Lara
↗ Midfielder ↗ El Nacional
↗ Born: April 27, 1980

Edwin Tenorio
↗ Midfielder ↗ Barcelona SC
↗ Born: June 16, 1976

THE ROAD TO THE FINALS

W 2-0	home v Venezuela (Espinoza, Tenorio)
L 0-1	away v Brazil
L 1-2	away v Paraguay (Mendez)
D 0-0	home v Peru
L 0-1	away v Argentina
W 2-1	home v Colombia (Delgado, Salas)
W 3-2	home v Bolivia (Solis, Delgado, De la Cruz)
L 0-1	away v Uruguay
W 2-0	home v Chile (Kaviedes, Mendez)
L 1-3	away v Venezuela (Ayovi)
W 1-0	home v Brazil (Mendez)
W 5-2	home v Paraguay (Valencia 2, Mendez 2, Ayovi)
D 2-2	away v Peru (De la Cruz, Valencia)
W 2-0	home v Argentina (Lara, Delgado)
L 0-3	away v Colombia
W 2-1	away v Bolivia (Delgado 2)
D 0-0	home v Uruguay
D 0-0	away v Chile

COACH

Luis Fernando Suarez
↗ Born: March 4, 1954 ↗ Appointed August 2004
↗ Previous: Colombia youth

STAR PLAYER

Augustin Delgado
↗ Striker ↗ Barcelona SC (Ecuador)
↗ Born: December 23, 1974
"Tin" Delgado made history at the last World Cup by scoring Ecuador's first-ever finals goals. Career travels have included spells in Mexico (Cruz Azul, Necaxa and Pumas) and England (Southampton).

ENGLAND

SVEN'S MOMENT OF TRUTH

Wayne Rooney inspires dreams of England's glory as the 1966 World Cup winners bid to end 40 lean years. But Sven-Goran Eriksson and his midfield trio need to work at building a perfect platform on which the United striker can deliver the goods.

Even Sven-Goran Eriksson's bitterest critics tend to agree on one good reason why his England team could just win the World Cup in 2006: the answer is not the dapper Swedish manager himself but the 20-year-old Wayne Rooney.

The Manchester United striker has established himself as one of the world's most famous and feared strikers. In Eriksson's words: "He has such talent he can do whatever he wants."

Rooney's four goals in three games at Euro 2004 and a Champions League debut hat-trick for United demonstrated how he thrives on the big occasion. Now he approaches the biggest of them all, in Germany.

Strangely, the former Everton wonderboy did not contribute a single goal to England's qualifying campaign. Instead, the five-goal, top-scoring hero as England scraped through one of the easier European groups was Chelsea midfielder Frank Lampard.

Perhaps predictably, though, Rooney and David Beckham provided the most memorable moments of a mixed-up campaign, albeit all too often for negative reasons.

Beckham spoiled the effect of a wondrous goal in a 2–0 win over Wales by deliberately provoking a yellow card so he would miss the next game in Azerbaijan. FIFA president Sepp Blatter and England's 1966 hat-trick hero Sir Geoff Hurst were among those who condemned the captain who thought – initially, at least – that he was being "clever".

Beckham then missed the final group match after a red card for two bookings in two minutes against Austria. Rooney was missing from that match, having been booked against Northern Ireland before redirecting his verbal abuse from the referee towards his surprised captain.

England's hopes of winning Euro 2004 began to evaporate as soon as Rooney limped out of the quarter-final against Portugal. If he goes missing in Germany, whether through injury or suspension, then England will surely struggle again to maintain both morale and creativity.

The 1–0 defeat by Northern Ireland, England's first upset in Belfast in 78 years, was the lowest point of a mischievous season for Eriksson. Few had expected England to lose to their neighbours, deep down the FIFA world rankings. Yet warning signs were evident in the 4–1 friendly loss to Denmark in August as well as a scrappy 1–0 win in Wales.

These three poor performances increased the pressure not only on the

WORLD CUP RECORD

1930 ineligible	1974 did not qualify
1934 ineligible	1978 did not qualify
1938 ineligible*	1982 2nd round
1950 1st round	1986 quarter-finals
1954 quarter-finals	1990 fourth place
1958 1st round	1994 did not qualify
1962 quarter-finals	1998 2nd round
1966 champions	2002 quarter-finals
1970 quarter-finals	

*England, though outside FIFA, rejected a late invitation to compete after the withdrawal of Austria

STAR PERFORMERS

John Terry
↗ Central defender ↗ Chelsea
↗ Born: December 7, 1980

Frank Lampard
↗ Midfielder ↗ Chelsea
↗ Born: June 20, 1978

Steven Gerrard
↗ Midfielder ↗ Liverpool
↗ Born: May 30, 1980

David Beckham
↗ Midfielder ↗ Real Madrid
↗ Born: May 2, 1975

Michael Owen
↗ Striker ↗ Newcastle United
↗ Born: December 14, 1979

THE ROAD TO THE FINALS

D 2-2	away v Austria (Lampard, Gerrard)
W 2-1	away v Poland (Defoe, Glowacki og)
W 2-0	home v Wales (Lampard, Beckham)
W 1-0	away v Azerbaijan (Owen)
W 4-0	home v Northern Ireland (Cole, Owen, Baird og, Lampard)
W 2-0	home v Azerbaijan (Gerrard, Beckham)
W 1-0	away v Wales (J Cole)
L 0-1	away v Northern Ireland
W 1-0	home v Austria (Lampard)
W 2-1	home v Poland (Owen, Lampard)

LEFT: David Beckham who scored two goals in the qualifiers for England in a welcome return to form.

COACH

Sven-Goran Eriksson

↗ Born: February 9, 1948

Injury made Eriksson quit early as a player and turn to coaching with success both at home with IFK Gothenburg and abroad with Benfica (Portugal) and Sampdoria, Roma, Fiorentina and Lazio (Italy). In 2001 he succeeded Kevin Keegan, becoming the first foreigner to manage England. Within months he was celebrating the sensational 5–1 win over Germany in Munich.

highly paid superstars of the over-hyped Premiership but also on Eriksson, who was variously pilloried by critics taking turns in attacking his lavish salary, his tactics and suspected devotion to "favourites" such as Beckham.

After experimenting with a diamond formation at Euro 2004, Eriksson had suddenly switched to 4-5-1 in Wales and Northern Ireland. This offered Beckham the role of holding midfielder or, as the skipper grandly styled himself, "quarterback".

But this also deprived England of his pinpoint crosses from the right wing, while confusing, rather than helping, both Lampard and Steven Gerrard.

These players are arguably two of the best central midfielders in Europe. Yet despite Jose Mourinho's vain attempts to unite them at Chelsea, the pair have struggled to dovetail for England.

Both are exuberant players who enjoy bursting forward into goalscoring positions. For England, however, neither seemed sure when to push forward or when to stay back. The debate over their partnership, team tactics and who fills the left-wing role promises to run right up until England's opening match in Germany.

At least Eriksson is well served in defence. Paul Robinson, after replacing David James as England's number one, kept six clean sheets in qualifying.

Ahead of him Sol Campbell and Rio Ferdinand had already proved themselves as one of the most rock-solid centre-back pairings at the 2002 World Cup. Both hope for a repeat in Germany even though one will have to make way for the formidable Chelsea captain John Terry.

Michael Owen's return to the Premiership with Newcastle last autumn from the substitutes' bench at Real Madrid was expected to provide him with the platform to secure a role as Rooney's unchallenged attacking partner.

Owen, apart from his eye for goal, posseses invaluable World Cup experience after his successes both as a teenager in France in 1998 and then again in Korea and Japan in 2002.

On both occasions, however, England's failure to progress beyond, respectively, the second round and the quarter-finals meant they flew home amid a distinct air of anti-climax. A similar sense of déjà vu followed the subsequent quarter-final failure at Euro 2004.

England, World Cup winners back in 1966 and semi-finalists in 1990, often shoulder a weight of domestic and media expectation beyond the bounds of reality.

But, if nothing else in Germany, then the travelling faithful will expect, at the very least, that Eriksson's men will not fail this time for any lack of expertise from the penalty spot.

STAR PLAYER

Wayne Rooney

↗ Striker ↗ Manchester United

↗ Born: October 24, 1985

Rooney's striking fame preceded him even ahead of his Everton debut at 16 and his spectacular winning goal against Arsenal two months later. He had become England's youngest-ever debutant and youngest-ever goalscorer by the time his exploits at Euro 2004 turned him into an international superstar. He scored two goals apiece in victories over Switzerland and Croatia and his instant impact was compared with that of Pele at the 1958 World Cup in Sweden. Within weeks of returning home Rooney had been sold to Manchester United for £28million. He failed to score in the World Cup qualifiers but said it was merely because he was "saving them all up for the finals".

PARAGUAY

HARD TO BEAT

Paraguay look to Justo Villar, the new Jose Luis Chilavert, to drive them forward towards their "usual" place in the second round – and then maybe a little further – after another crazy, mixed-up South American qualifying campaign.

Whenever they take part in the World Cup finals, Paraguay invariably leave their legacy in some shape or form.

Eight years ago in France, inspired by eccentric goalkeeper Jose Luis Chilavert, the Paraguayans fell victim only to Laurent Blanc's golden goal, which prevented a potential upset of massive proportions and spared the host nation's blushes.

On the way to that crucial second-round clash, the South Americans had beaten hotly favoured Nigeria and they returned home with a growing reputation.

Four years later they again emerged from the group stage, this time earning a date with eventual runners-up Germany. Chilavert and his veteran defence delivered yet another valiant display, but again fell just short.

Being hard to beat has traditionally been seen as Paraguay's main attribute, but this was certainly not the case at the start of their qualifying campaign for 2006, when they were thumped 4–1 by Peru back in September 2003. Four days later, in Asuncion, they confounded their critics when they defeated Uruguay by the same score, thus setting in motion a maddening unpredictability that was the hallmark of their entire campaign.

Initially, the *Albirroja* struggled and 2004 saw just one win from seven outings. Eventually they just did enough to clinch fourth spot in the final table with an identical goals for and goals against tally. Yet their home fans were unimpressed and the Germany-bound players found themselves booed off after a 1–0 defeat in their final home game against Colombia.

No-one should underestimate Paraguay's World Cup ambitions, however. The main plus from their erratic campaign was the emergence of a talented crop of youngsters, with goalkeeper Justo Villar at the top of the list as a worthy successor to Chilavert, captain in both 1998 and 2002.

At the other end of the pitch, Nelson Haedo Valdez, who scored the goal in Venezuela which sent his side to Germany, will need constant attention from opposing defences.

Paraguay expect now to reach the knockout round for the third consecutive time. After that everything depends on the balance they achieve between the new young guns and the veterans.

WORLD CUP RECORD

1930 1st round	1974 did not qualify
1934 did not enter	1978 did not qualify
1938 did not enter	1982 did not qualify
1950 1st round	1986 2nd round
1954 did not enter	1990 did not qualify
1958 1st round	1994 did not qualify
1962 did not qualify	1998 2nd round
1966 did not qualify	2002 2nd round
1970 did not qualify	

STAR PERFORMERS

Carlos Alberto Gamarra
↗ Central defender ↗ Internazionale
↗ Born: February 17, 1971

Salvador Cabanas
↗ Forward ↗ Jaguares
↗ Born: August 5, 1980

Denis Caniza
↗ Defender ↗ Santos Laguna
↗ Born: August 20, 1974

Nelson Haedo Valdez
↗ Forward ↗ Werder Bremen
↗ Born: November 28, 1983

Roque Santa Cruz
↗ Forward ↗ Bayern Munich
↗ Born: August 16, 1981

COACH

Anibal Ruiz
↗ Born: December 30, 1942 ↗ Appointed: April 2003 ↗ Previous: Atletico Nacional (Colombia), Pueblo, Leon (Mexico), El Salvador, Uruguay

THE ROAD TO THE FINALS

L 1-4	away v Peru (Gamarra)
W 4-1	home v Uruguay (Cardozo 3, Paredes)
W 2-1	home v Ecuador (Santa Cruz, Cardozo)
W 1-0	away v Chile (Paredes)
D 0-0	home v Brazil
L 1-2	away v Bolivia (Cardozo)
D 0-0	away v Argentina
W 1-0	home v Venezuela (Gamarra)
D 1-1	away v Colombia (Gavilan)
D 1-1	home v Peru (Paredes)
L 0-1	away v Uruguay
L 2-5	away v Ecuador (Cardozo, Cabanas)
W 2-1	home v Chile (Morinigo, Cardozo)
L 1-4	away v Brazil (Santa Cruz)
W 4-1	home v Bolivia (Gamarra, Santa Cruz, J C Caceres, Nunez)
W 1—0	home v Argentina (Santa Cruz)
W 1-0	away v Venezuela (Haedo Valdez)
L 0-1	home v Colombia

STAR PLAYER

Justo Villar
↗ Goalkeeper ↗ Libertad
↗ Born: June 30, 1977

Villar has taken on the mantle of larger-than-life Jose Luis Chilavert in the Paraguayan goal after starring with Sol de America and Libertad. Decided to be a goalkeeper so he could follow in his father's footsteps.

TRINIDAD & TOBAGO

A TOUCH OF SUNSHINE

Dwight Yorke finds himself back on the international stage with island newcomers as Leo Beenhakker's Soca Warriors prepare to emulate the Reggae Boys and warm up the World Cup finals with their own brand of Caribbean sunshine.

First the Reggae Boys from Jamaica, now the Soca Warriors from Trinidad and Tobago. You do not have to be a genius to work out which country will be everyone's second favourite team in Germany.

When qualifying began in the North, Central American and Caribbean zone, it was always likely that the traditional powers of Mexico, the United States and Costa Rica would grab the three automatic berths. But in a sport which thrives on unpredictability, it was left to Trinidad and Tobago to defy the odds and book their ticket as well after a nerve-jangling play-off win over Bahrain.

Not even their most diehard fans gave Trinidad – a nation where football has always had a massive following but where cricket is the sport with the pedigree – much of a chance of reaching Germany, yet there can be no denying they earned their place on merit, thanks in no small measure to Leo Beenhakker.

The wily Dutch coach's timely arrival rescued a team whose qualifying hopes were hanging by a thread before he somehow managed to lead them into the play-offs and a hard-fought win over Bahrain, after they had come fourth out of six teams in the qualifiers.

With the tie delicately poised at 1–1 following the jittery first home leg, the Soca Warriors showed they had nerves of steel to snatch the 1–0 away win which sent them to their first-ever World Cup finals.

For Dwight Yorke, the country's most famous player, the finals will provide an opportunity to go out on the biggest stage of all. The same can be said for the team's creative hero Russell Latapy, aka "The Little Magician", who, at 37, must have thought that his chance to strut his stuff alongside the global elite had gone.

Germany will also see the former Nottingham Forest and Birmingham City striker Stern John, top scorer with 12 goals in qualifying, determined to prove he can mix it with the best.

Last summer few people would have been willing to bet on this tiny nation of 1.1 million people even qualifying. What are the odds now on marking their finals debut with a win over some unsuspecting giant?

WORLD CUP RECORD

1930-62 did not exist	1986 did not qualify
1966 did not qualify	1990 did not qualify
1970 did not qualify	1994 did not qualify
1974 did not qualify	1998 did not qualify
1978 did not qualify	2002 did not qualify
1982 did not qualify	

STAR PERFORMERS

Shaka Hislop
↗ Goalkeeper ↗ West Ham United
↗ Born: February 22, 1969

Dennis Lawrence
↗ Central defender ↗ Wrexham
↗ Born: August 1, 1974

Chris Birchall
↗ Midfield ↗ Port Vale
↗ Born: May 5, 1984

Russell Latapy
↗ Midfield ↗ Falkirk
↗ Born: August 2, 1968

Stern John
↗ Striker ↗ Coventry City
↗ Born: October 30, 1976

COACH

Leo Beenhakker
↗ Born: August 2, 1942 ↗ Appointed: May 2005
↗ Previous: Go Ahead Eagles, Ajax, Zaragoza (Spain), Holland, Real Madrid (Spain), Ajax, Holland, Real Madrid, Grasshopper (Switzerland), Saudi Arabia, America (Mexico), Istanbulspor (Turkey), Feyenoord, Ajax

THE ROAD TO THE FINALS

1st round	
W 2-0	away v Dominican Rep (Andrews, John)
W 4-0	home v Dominican Rep (Scotland, John, Theobald, Sealy)
2nd round	
W 2-0	away v St Vincent & Grenadines (McFarlane 2)
W 2-1	away v St Kitts & Nevis (McFarlane, John)
L 1-3	home v Mexico (John)
W 5-1	home v St Kitts & Nevis (Riley, John 2, Glenn, Nixon)
L 0-3	away v Mexico
W 2-1	home v St Vincent & Grenadines (Sam, Eve)
3rd round	
L 1-2	home v United States (Eve)
L 1-5	away v Guatemala (Edwards)
D 0-0	home v Costa Rica
W 2-0	home v Panama (John, Lawrence)
L 0-2	away v Mexico
L 0-1	away v United States
W 3-2	home v Guatemala (Latapy, John 2)
L 0-2	away v Costa Rica
W 1-0	away v Panama (John)
W 2-1	home v Mexico (John 2)
Play-off	
D 1-1	home v Bahrain (Birchall)
W 1-0	away v Bahrain (Lawrence)
Trinidad & Tobago 2-1 on agg	

STAR PLAYER

Dwight Yorke
↗ Striker ↗ Sydney FC
↗ Born: November 3, 1971
Yorke was discovered by Graham Taylor, then Aston Villa boss, on a tour to Trinidad 1989. A free-scoring start earned a £12.6m move to Manchester United and he was a key figure in the club which won the 1999 treble.

SWEDEN

HAIL THE NEW BREED

Henrik Larsson and Zlatan Ibrahimovic conjure up a mixture of the old and the new in attack as Lars Lagerback's Sweden threaten the favourites once more with a mixture of established stalwarts and bright new heroes.

Coach Lars Lagerback is confident that a new generation of attacking stars can continue Sweden's proud record in the World Cup finals.

The Swedes finished third in 1950, were runners-up to Brazil on home soil eight years later and beat Bulgaria 4–0 in the third-place play-off in 1994. Henrik Larsson, the man who scored the third goal, is the only survivor from that squad.

Larsson, now 34, will play in his third World Cup finals in Germany. He put Sweden ahead in their last game in the finals, against Senegal in the 2002 last 16, only to see Henri Camara level then score the extra-time decider.

Larsson lacked support in the absence of the injured Freddie Ljungberg, who is expected to attack from behind the two strikers in Germany, in contrast to his wide role for Arsenal.

Sweden have a new hero up front, too, in Zlatan Ibrahimovic. The former Malmo and Ajax striker was a substitute against Senegal. Now the Juventus star is Sweden's Player of the Year and topped their scoring list with eight goals in the qualifiers, ahead of Ljungberg (seven) and Larsson (five).

He scored a vital stoppage-time winner against Hungary in Budapest. Then he netted the equaliser which set the Swedes on their way to the 3–1 win over Iceland which clinched qualification.

Ibrahimovic's Juve colleague, Czech midfielder Pavel Nedved, believes he could make a big impact in Germany. Nedved says: "Zlatan has a lot more in his locker yet. He could do even better than Andriy Shevchenko."

Ibrahimovic played second fiddle to Larsson at Euro 2004. A month after the competition, he announced his international arrival by making one goal, then scoring the equaliser, as Sweden drew 2–2 against their Euro 2004 conquerors Holland.

Lagerback believes the 23-year-old striker's progress heralds the rise of a new generation. The coach said: "That's been the trend in Sweden in the last few years. We have several young players coming through in midfield and the forward positions."

Rennes midfielder Kim Kallstrom, Anderlecht winger Christian Wilhelmsson, Brondby striker Johan Elmander and Ajax forward Markus Rosenberg offer more attacking options. So does the pacy Tobias Hysen, the star of Djurgardens' domestic double success. He was called up for last November's 2–2 friendly draw against South Korea, when Elmander and Rosenberg netted Sweden's goals.

BELOW: Freddie Ljungberg is expected to play in the crucial support role behind Sweden's front two.

WORLD CUP RECORD

1930 did not enter	1974 2nd round
1934 quarter-finals	1978 1st round
1938 fourth place	1982 did not qualify
1950 third place	1986 did not qualify
1954 did not qualify	1990 1st round
1958 runners-up	1994 third place
1962 did not qualify	1998 did not qualify
1966 did not qualify	2002 2nd round
1970 1st round	

STAR PERFORMERS

Andreas Isaksson
↗ Goalkeeper ↗ Rennes
↗ Born: October 3, 1981

Teddy Lucic
↗ Defender ↗ BK Hacken
↗ Born: April 15, 1973

Olof Mellberg
↗ Central defender ↗ Aston Villa
↗ Born: September 3, 1977

Fredrik Ljungberg
↗ Forward ↗ Arsenal
↗ Born: April 16, 1977

Henrik Larsson
↗ Striker ↗ Barcelona
↗ Born: September 20, 1971

THE ROAD TO THE FINALS

W 7-0	away v Malta (Ibrahimovic 4, Ljungberg 2, Larsson)
L 0-1	home v Croatia
W 3-0	home v Hungary (Ljungberg, Larsson, A Svensson)
W 4-1	away v Iceland (Larsson 2, Wilhelmsson, Allback)
W 3-0	away v Bulgaria (Ljungberg 2, Edman)
W 6-0	home v Malta (M Jonson, A Svensson, Wilhelmsson, Ibrahimovic, Ljungberg, Elmander)
W 3-0	home v Bulgaria (Ljunberg, Mellberg, Ibrahimovic)
W 1-0	away v Hungary (Ibrahimovic)
L 0-1	away v Croatia
W 3-1	home v Iceland (Ibrahimovic, Larsson, Kallstrom)

STAR PLAYER

Zlatan Ibrahimovic

↗ Striker ↗ Juventus

↗ Born: October 3, 1981

Ibrahimovic is the current Swedish Footballer of the Year after crucial goals in Sweden's qualifying campaign and Juventus' 2005 Italian league title win. Born in Malmo of Bosnian immigrant parents, "Ibra" played for a local ethnic club called FBK Balkan before turning professional with Malmo in 1999. The club rejected a bid from Arsenal but accepted a later £5m deal with Ajax. After a slow start, Ibrahimovic blossomed in Amsterdam under the management of Ronald Koeman. He scored 36 league goals in just over three seasons and was sold for a club record £11m to Juventus in the summer of 2004, a matter of hours before the close of the transfer window.

Another relative youngster, the 24-year-old Rennes keeper Andreas Isaksson, has established himself as his country's number one.

Sweden have plenty of old heads too. Skipper Olof Mellberg, the Aston Villa centre-back, and ex-Leeds defender Teddy Lucic are both veterans of 2002. So are midfielders Anders Svensson and Niclas Alexandersson, anchor man Tobias Linderoth and striker Marcus Allback.

Feyenoord's Alex Ostlund and former Tottenham defender Erik Edman offer more experience in a settled back line on either side of Mellberg and Lucic.

The Swedes won eight of their 10 qualifiers and netted 30 goals. Thirteen came in two victories over Malta. But Lagerback would prefer to stress the 17 scored in the other eight games. He says: "That's good, isn't it? I'm pleased with the players. They've shown really good character and attacked very well."

The coach believes his side proved their quality by winning four of their five away matches, losing only to Darijo Srna's penalty for Croatia in Zagreb. Larsson netted twice in a 4–1 success in Iceland. Ljungberg's opener sparked a 3–0 win over Bulgaria.

Sweden showed resilience as well, to win in Budapest four days later. Lagerback said: "We were very good against Bulgaria but the Hungary match was more about battling. They played with five, sometimes six midfielders. We had to compete with them. We hung in and won with a very good goal at the end."

Yet Sweden qualified for the finals only as one of the top runners-up. They finished level on points with Croatia in group eight, but lost twice to them.

Lagerback refuses to read any significance into those results, especially the 1–0 defeat in Gothenburg. Srna scored the only goal of a bad-tempered match from a 63rd-minute free kick and Ibrahimovic had an equaliser controversially disallowed.

"Croatia were lucky to win," says Lagerback with considerable conviction. "They did a job tactically and closed down fast when they lost the ball. We created some good chances and, if anyone looked like winning that game, it was us."

He knows, however, that World Cup rivals are likely to employ similar tactics to frustrate and upset his team. How Sweden respond to that lesson may determine how far their gifted squad advance.

COACH

Lars Lagerback

↗ Born: July 16, 1948

Lagerback has been national boss for five years, having initially worked in tandem with Tommy Sodberg for three years. After a playing career with minor clubs Alby and Gimonas, Lagerback coached in the lower divisions before joining the federation staff in 1990. Managed the youth and B teams before becoming Soderberg's assistant in 1999 and then partner in 2000.

ARGENTINA

A QUESTION OF CONFIDENCE

Argentina's breadth of footballing talent has established them as the reigning Olympic and World Youth champions. But an even greater challenge facing coach Jose Pekerman is how to transform outstanding ability into achievement at this World Cup.

Argentina go to the World Cup finals determined not only to win but to prove that they, and not Brazil, are South America's top footballing nation.

The Argentines lost on penalties to Brazil in the 2004 Copa America final and lost to them again – by a 4–1 margin – in the final of the Confederations Cup in Frankfurt's redeveloped Waldstadion last summer. In between, however, they had the satisfaction of beating the old enemy 3–1 in the World Cup qualifiers to seal their place in the finals.

Victory in the World Cup would emulate the hat-tricks of not only Brazil but also of Italy and Germany and throw off the long shadow cast by the achievements of Diego Maradona, which still intimidate Argentine players today.

Of course "El Dieguito" is a tough act to follow. He was considered too inexperienced by then manager Cesar Luis Menotti to join in the 1978 World Cup victory, but he was captain and a mischievous inspiration in 1986 when, against England, he scored one of the most notorious and then one of the most spectacular goals in finals history.

ABOVE: Javier Zanetti is one his country's most versatile players, operating in defence or midfield.

Argentina hailed both his audacity and sublime talent and have long since forgiven him for the subsequent cocaine-soaked years of scandal. After self-imposed curative exile in Cuba then surgery to control his ballooning weight, Maradona returned to Argentina to regain his old pre-eminence in the media and the game.

This means he goes wherever the national team go and he draws more cheers and acclaim from fans than many of the present heroes. Stepping out from Maradona's shadow is all part of the double-edged World Cup challenge.

Coach Jose Nestor Pekerman was promoted from his favoured role as youth team boss to succeed Marcelo Bielsa after Argentina's Olympic Games-winning performance in Athens in the summer of 2004. His first challenge was to sort out the tactics.

Though Pekerman is an advocate of 4-4-2 and imposed that legacy on his youth teams, Argentina's seniors have generally played 3-5-2 ever since it was devised by then boss Carlos Bilardo on the way to victory in the Mexico World Cup of 1986. Asked for his preference, Pekerman always insists that the guiding factor must be the players available – which is why 3-5-2 is often the choice.

Attacking wing-backs such as Javier Zanetti and Juan Pablo Sorin are World Cup veterans with defensive talent but also technique and pace which is the envy of many forwards. This offers them the ability to support the attack but retreat quickly into defensive roles when Argentina come under fire.

Roberto Ayala and Walter Samuel comprise an experienced partnership

WORLD CUP RECORD

1930 runners-up	1974 2nd round
1934 1st round	1978 champions
1938 did not enter	1982 2nd round
1950 did not enter	1986 champions
1954 did not enter	1990 runners-up
1958 1st round	1994 2nd round
1962 1st round	1998 quarter-finals
1966 quarter-final	2002 1st round
1970 did not qualify	

STAR PERFORMERS

Javier Zanetti
↗ Right-back ↗ Internazionale
↗ Born: August 10, 1973

Roberto Fabian Ayala
↗ Central defender ↗ Valencia
↗ Born: April 14, 1973

Juan Pablo Sorin
↗ Wing-back/midfielder ↗ Villarreal
↗ Born: May 5, 1976

Juan Roman Riquelme
↗ Midfielder ↗ Villarreal
↗ Born: June 26, 1978

Lionel "Leo" Messi
↗ Forward ↗ Barcelona ↗ Born: June 24, 1987

THE ROAD TO THE FINALS

D 2-2	home v Chile (Kily Gonzalez, Aimar)
W 3-0	away v Venezuela (Aimar, Crespo, Delgado)
W 3-0	home v Bolivia (D'Alessandro, Crespo, Aimar)
D 1-1	away v Colombia (Crespo)
W 1-0	home v Ecuador (Crespo)
L 1-3	away v Brazil (Sorin)
D 0-0	home v Paraguay
W 3-1	away v Peru (Rosales, Coloccini, Sorin)
W 4-2	home v Uruguay (L Gonzalez, Figueroa 2, Zanetti)
D 0-0	away v Chile
W 3-2	home v Venezuela (Rey og, Riquelme, Saviola)
W 2-1	away v Bolivia (Figueroa, Galletti)
W 1-0	home v Colombia (Crespo)
L 0-2	away v Ecuador
W 3-1	home v Brazil (Crespo 2, Riquelme)
L 0-1	away v Paraguay
W 2-0	home v Peru (Riquelme, Guadalupe)
L 0-1	away v Uruguay

STAR PLAYER

Hernan Crespo

↗ Centre-forward ↗ Chelsea ↗ Born: July 5, 1975

Crespo made his name in Argentina in the early 1990s with River Plate where fans nicknamed him "Valdanito" for his resemblance to the 1986 World Cup winner. He scored 13 goals in his first full season to help River win the league title and earn promotion to the national team with whom he made his debut in a 4–1 win over Bulgaria in February 1995. The following year Crespo led Argentina to Olympic silver medal status in Atlanta, helped River win the South American Copa Libertadores and moved to Italy, first with Parma then with Lazio – with whom he won the Italian Cup and European Cup-Winners' Cup. Crespo was subsequently sold to Internazionale , joined Chelsea in 2002, was then loaned to Milan in 2003, before returning to west London in 2005.

at the heart of defence with the energetic Esteban Cambiasso or Jorge D'Alessandro available to guide the attacking strategy from midfield.

What happens next depends on the creative wanderings of playmakers such as Juan Roman Riquelme, Juan Sebastian Veron and Juan Pablo Aimar and then the striking talents of Hernan Crespo, Javier Saviola and their skilful co-workers and competitors.

Pekerman says: "We have all the necessary players with the qualities to take us a very long way at the World Cup: a winning mentality, aggression, tactical discipline, technical ability to keep possession. But then other factors come into play such as players' fitness after a long European season. A winning football team is very much a delicately tuned machine."

The unknown factor is whether teenage superstar Leo Messi will be able to rise to the occasion. Messi, brought to Europe at 13 by Barcelona, was the top-scoring inspiration of Argentina's World Youth Cup triumph in Holland last summer. He was instantly propelled into the senior side but made headlines of the wrong sort after being sent off for an elbowing offence two minutes after the kick-off on his debut against Hungary in Budapest.

Top Italian coach Fabio Capello went as far as to describe Messi as "the best 17-year-old I have ever seen", which is praise indeed from a man who has both played alongside and managed some of the finest footballers of the modern era. The crucial unanswered question concerns experience and whether Pekerman will consider Messi capable of withstanding the pressures already accumulating from over-hyped labels such as "the new Maradona".

The psychological state of Argentina's players is crucial. They need not lack for world-beating confidence: Argentina are Olympic and World Youth champions and boast a World Cup-winning pedigree.

But confidence abounded as they approached the 2002 World Cup in South Korea and Japan . . . and then they had to fly home after "only" the first round.

COACH

Jose Nestor Pekerman

↗ Born: September 3, 1949

Pekerman, never an international, played out a journeyman's career with Argentinos Juniors and Independiente Medellin in Colombia. He then worked as a taxi driver and ice cream salesman before being offered his first youth coaching post back with Argentinos Juniors. His success took him on to the federation staff and he guided Argentina to three world junior cups before succeeding Marcelo Bielsa as senior boss after the 2002 World Cup.

IVORY COAST

GREAT EXPECTATIONS

Ivory Coast's Elephants are ready to trumpet their progress around the world after capitalizing on Cameroon's blunders to reach the finals for the first time thanks to the goal-hungry duo of Didier Drogba and Aruna Dindane.

Ivory Coast's first-ever qualification for the World Cup finals hinged on a last-minute penalty – for Cameroon.

Lens striker Aruna Dindane had scored twice as Ivory Coast's "Elephants" won their final game 3–1 against Sudan in Omdurman. But victory for Cameroon over Egypt in Yaounde would have taken them to Germany instead. The score was 1–1 when Cameroon were awarded a spot kick four minutes into stoppage time. Pierre Wome missed the penalty and Ivory Coast thus finished a point ahead of their west African rivals.

Cameroon's demise had seemed an unlikely outcome after they won 3–2 in the Ivory Coast capital, Abidjan, in the penultimate qualifier – Achille Webo's hat-trick trumping Chelsea striker Didier Drogba's two for the home side.

Mighty Cameroon had also beaten Ivory Coast 2–0 in Yaounde. But they paid the penalty for taking it easy against some of the lesser teams in the group. They drew three matches and lost 3–2 in Egypt, while Ivory Coast dropped only one point in their other eight games.

While the inquest raged in Cameroon, Ivory Coast celebrated, even in the rebel-held north of the country. Football federation president Jacques Anouma used the Elephants' triumph to plead for national unity. He said: "The players want this success to make our divided country one again. This must bring us together."

Drogba, who hit nine goals in the qualifiers, dedicated victory to assistant coach Mama Ouattara, who died in June 2004. Drogba and Dindane, who scored seven, are an intimidating duo up front. They netted all but four of Ivory Coast's 20 goals in qualifying. The team and their veteran French coach Henri Michel celebrated by downing a new brand of beer named Drogba in honour of the Chelsea striker.

The Ivorians field other Europe-based stars – the Arsenal defender Kolo Toure, Paris Saint-Germain midfielder Bonaventure Kalou and Messina defender Marc Zoro.

But Chelsea striker Drogba's partnership with Dindane offers the Elephants their best hope of trampling on a few unsuspecting opponents in Germany.

STAR PERFORMERS

Kolo Toure
↗ Central defender ↗ Arsenal
↗ Born: March 19, 1981

Bonaventure Kalou
↗ Midfielder ↗ Paris Saint-Germain
↗ January 12, 1978

Didier Zokora
↗ Midfielder ↗ Saint-Etienne
↗ Born: December 14, 1980

Bakary Kone
↗ Forward ↗ Nice
↗ Born: September 17, 1981

Aruna Dindane
↗ Striker ↗ Lens ↗ Born: November 26, 1980

COACH

Henri Michel
↗ Born: October 28, 1947 ↗ Appointed: October 2003
↗ Previous: France U21s, France, Morocco, Cameroon

THE ROAD TO THE FINALS

1st round – bye

2nd round

W 2-0	home v Libya (Dindane, Drogba)
W 2-1	away v Egypt (Dindane, Drogba)
L 0-2	away v Cameroon
W 5-0	home v Sudan (Drogba, Dindane 2, Yapi, Kone)
W 1-0	away v Benin (Dindane)
W 3-0	home v Benin (B Kalou, Drogba 2)
D 0-0	away v Libya
W 2-0	home v Egypt (Drogba 2)
L 2-3	home v Cameroon (Drogba 2)
W 3-1	away v Sudan (Akale, Dindane 2)

WORLD CUP RECORD

1930-58 did not exist	1986 did not qualify
1962-70 did not enter	1990 did not qualify
1974 did not qualify	1994 did not qualify
1978 did not qualify	1998 did not qualify
1982 did not qualify	2002 did not qualify

STAR PLAYER

Didier Drogba
↗ Striker ↗ Chelsea
↗ Born: March 11, 1978

Drogba was born in Abidjan but brought up in France. He learned his football with Le Mans and Guingamp, before exploding on to the national and international scene with Marseille. He joined Chelsea for £24m in 2004.

SERBIA & MONTENEGRO

KINGS OF THE CLEAN SHEET

Mateja Kezman will lead the goal chase as the new-look Serbs make a tactical change for the better. Defensive discipline was the key to qualifying success. Now boss Ilija Petkovic wants to open up and put his new country firmly on the soccer map.

WORLD CUP RECORD

1930 semi-finals	1974 2nd round
1934 did not qualify	1978 did not qualify
1938 did not qualify	1982 1st round
1950 1st round	1986 did not qualify
1954 quarter-finals	1990 did not qualify
1958 quarter-finals	1994 did not qualify
1962 fourth place	1998 2nd round
1966 did not qualify	2002 did not qualify
1970 did not qualify	

(known as Yugoslavia until 2003)

Eight years after the former Yugoslavia last appeared in the World Cup finals, Serbia and Montenegro – the two remaining republics from the old federation – are back in the spotlight, smaller in size but no less passionate about their footballing heritage.

To finish ahead of Spain in Group Seven of the qualifying competition was no mean feat, a tribute to the powerful influence of coach Ilija Petkovic. While not blessed with as much individual talent as the Yugoslav team beaten by Holland in the last 16 in 1998, the two republics have proved stubborn and hard-nosed opponents in the build-up to Germany.

Petkovic, once a strong advocate of 3-5-2, saw a switch to 4-4-2 for the 2006 qualifiers reap dividends. Although the attacking star of the show is Atletico Madrid's Mateja Kezman, it is the Serb defence which won the most plaudits, conceding only one goal in 10 qualifying matches.

"I have built one team and one defence from the moment I became coach," says Petkovic with no little pride. "They work brilliantly with Mladen Krstajic in charge. Being settled is very important. If you keep a clean sheet, you cannot lose."

Cutting out prima donna instincts was another crucial element. Petkovic says: "Replacing stars like Stojkovic, Mijatovic and Savicevic proved impossible. So I decided to change the face of the team. I told my players: 'Stop being artists, you must become workers.'

"Now, the true secret of our success is we have got brilliant harmony among the whole squad."

Nothing illustrated local passion better than the final qualifier when Kezman's seventh-minute strike beat Balkan rivals Bosnia-Herzegovina to clinch a place in Germany.

The tie was played in Belgrade in an atmosphere highly charged with lingering resentments from the region's political and religious strife.

In Germany, however, such hostility will be put to one side. Serbia and Montenegro did not lose a single World Cup qualifier under Petkovic and confidence is high.

"What we have achieved hasn't sunk in yet," says skipper Krstajic. "We do not want to stop here, we want more glory days."

STAR PERFORMERS

Dragoslav Jevric
↗ Goalkeeper ↗ Ankaraspor
↗ Born: July 8, 1974

Goran Gavrancic
↗ Defender ↗ Dynamo Kiev
↗ Born: August 2, 1978

Mladen Krstajic
↗ Central defender ↗ Schalke
↗ Born: March 4, 1974

Nenad Jestrovic
↗ Striker ↗ Anderlecht
↗ Born: May 9, 1976

Dejan Stankovic
↗ Midfield ↗ Internazionale
↗ Born September 11, 1978

COACH

Ilija Petkovic
↗ Born: September 22, 1945 ↗ Appointed: July 2003
↗ Previous: Shanghai (China), OFK Belgrade, Yugoslavia, Servette (Switzerland)

STAR PLAYER

Mateja Kezman
↗ Striker ↗ Atletico Madrid
↗ Born: April 12, 1979

Kezman top-scored in the former Yugoslavia with Partizan Belgrade and then in Holland with PSV Eindhoven for whom he grabbed 81 goals in three seasons before a £5m move to Chelsea. He lasted only a year there, however.

THE ROAD TO THE FINALS

W 3-0	away v San Marino (Vukic, Jestrovic 2)
D 0-0	away v Bosnia-Herzegovina
W 5-0	home v San Marino (Milosevic, Stankovic 2, Koroman, Vukic)
W 2-0	away v Belgium (Vukic, Kezman)
D 0-0	home v Spain
D 0-0	home v Belgium
W 2-0	home v Lithuania (Kezman, Ilic)
D 1-1	away v Spain (Kezman)
W 2-0	away v Lithuania (Kezman, Vukic)
W 1-0	home v Bosnia-Herzegovina (Kezman)

HOLLAND

BRILLIANT ORANGE

Marco van Basten has proved he has Johan Cruyff's magic touch. The challenge now for Holland and their new boss is to go one better than the old Dutch master and win in Germany to make amends for the bitter memory of 1974.

Holland go to Germany among the favourites just like 32 years ago, when, inspired by Johan Cruyff, they reached the final but lost 2–1 to the hosts.

Four years later, in Argentina, the Dutch lost the final 3–1 in extra-time to the hosts. They have never touched such World Cup heights again. In 1994, they fell to Brazil, 3–2 in the quarter-finals. Four years later they lost to Brazil in a semi-final shoot-out after a 1–1 draw.

Penalties undid Holland again against 10-man Italy in the semi-finals of Euro 2000. The Dutch followed that by failing to qualify for the 2002 World Cup finals after the 1–0 defeat by 10-man Republic of Ireland that eventually cost coach Louis van Gaal his job.

Only once have Holland won a major trophy. That was in 1988, when Rinus Michels, coach of the 1974 squad, steered a team featuring Ruud Gullit, Ronald Koeman, Frank Rijkaard and Van Basten to the European crown.

Michels was, seemingly, the only coach down the years who could impose order in the dressing room. Bickering among themselves at major tournaments has become a Dutch trait. As 1974 World Cup finalist Wim van Hanegem said: "We think there's something strange if we don't have a problem."

Van Basten, top scorer at Euro 1988, succeeded Dick Advocaat as national coach after Holland lost to Portugal in the Euro 2004 semi-finals, his popularity overshadowing his lack of experience in the dugout.

He was widely seen as Cruyff's protégé. But he took a leaf out of Michels's book too, emphasising togetherness. After Holland beat the Czech Republic 2–0 in their opening qualifier, Van Basten said: "We played as a true team. It was so important that everyone did his job as we agreed."

He has rebuilt the squad since Euro 2004, casting aside the old guard – such as Michael Reiziger, Jaap Stam and Marc Overmars – and pointedly ignored the controversial likes of Clarence Seedorf and Patrick Kluivert.

Van Basten promoted the Hamburg defender Khalid Boulahrouz, AZ Alkmaar stalwarts Denny Landzaat and Barry Opdam and the Feyenoord attacker Dirk Kuyt. He encouraged youth in AZ defender Ron Vlaar, Ajax midfielders Hedwiges Maduro and Nigel de Jong and Arsenal forward Robin van Persie.

But a rich vein of experience still runs through the Dutch squad. Goalkeeper Edwin van der Sar has more than a century of caps; midfielder and skipper Philip Cocu is not far behind; Edgar "Pitbull" Davids, recalled in midfield for the final qualifiers, has close to 80 and left-back Gio van Bronckhorst more than 50.

ABOVE: In July 2004, flying winger Arjen Robben moved from PSV to Chelsea for £12million after turning down Manchester United.

WORLD CUP RECORD

1930 did not enter	1974 runners-up
1934 1st round	1978 runners-up
1938 1st round	1982 did not qualify
1950 did not enter	1986 did not qualify
1954 did not enter	1990 2nd round
1958 did not qualify	1994 quarter-finals
1962 did not qualify	1998 fourth place
1966 did not qualify	2002 did not qualify
1970 did not qualify	

STAR PERFORMERS

Edwin Van der Sar
↗ Goalkeeper ↗ Manchester United
↗ Born: October 29, 1970

Rafael Van der Vaart
↗ Midfielder ↗ Hamburg
↗ Born: February 11, 1983

Philip Cocu
↗ Midfielder ↗ PSV Eindhoven
↗ Born: October 29, 1970

Edgar Davids
↗ Midfielder ↗ Tottenham Hotspur
↗ Born: March 13, 1973

Arjen Robben
↗ Winger ↗ Chelsea ↗ Born: January 23, 1984

THE ROAD TO THE FINALS

W 2-0	home v Czech Republic (Van Hooijdonk 2)
D 2-2	away v Macedonia (Bouma, Kuijt)
W 3-1	home v Finland (Sneijder, Van Nistelrooy 2)
W 3-0	away v Andorra (Cocu, Robben, Sneijder)
W 2-0	away v Romania (Cocu, Babel)
W 2-0	home v Armenia (Castelen, Van Nistelrooy)
W 2-0	home v Romania (Robben, Kuijt)
W 4-0	away v Finland (Van Nistelrooy, Kuijt, Cocu, Van Persie)
W 1-0	away v Armenia (Van Nistelrooy)
W 4-0	home v Andorra (Van der Vaart, Cocu, Van Nistelrooy 2)
W 2-0	away v Czech Republic (Van der Vaart, Opdam)
D 0-0	home v Macedonia

COACH

Marco Van Basten

↗ Born: October 31, 1964

Van Basten ranks among the greatest of Dutch footballers after 24 goals in 58 games, including a wonder strike in the 1988 European Championship final. He was three times European Footballer of the Year but injury cut short his career with Ajax and Milan. He then progressed from Ajax youth coach to succeed Dick Advocaat as national coach in the summer of 2004.

STAR PLAYER

Ruud Van Nistelrooy

↗ Centre-forward ↗ Manchester United ↗ Born: July 1, 1976

Van Nistelrooy is a World Cup finals latecomer aiming to make up for lost time. The former PSV Eindhoven spearhead missed out in 1998 and then Holland failed to qualify in 2002. He missed Euro 2000 through injury and, thus, marked his big-stage debut with four goals in leading Holland to the Euro 2004 semi-finals. His hunger for World Cup goals was underlined by the nine he scored on the road to Germany. Simultaneously, his talent for rising to the international occasion is evident from the fact that Manchester United's £19million striker now ranks among the most prolific marksmen in the history of the European Champions Cup.

Like Cruyff, however, Van Basten can often surprise. Before the crucial qualifier away to the Czechs, he named a 33-man squad and challenged players to earn places in the starting line-up.

Van Basten's call drew an eager response from Rafael van der Vaart. He found the form of his life for Hamburg, forced his way back into the side and shot the first goal in Holland's 2–0 win. Van Basten said: "If we want to have a good World Cup, then we have to beat opponents like the Czech Republic. This was the perfect opportunity and we took it."

The Dutch have thrived under his leadership. They rose to second in the FIFA world rankings after dominating European Group One qualifying from start to finish. They won 10 games and drew two against Macedonia, the second after qualification was assured. They clinched their place in Germany with that win in Prague when Van der Sar saved a penalty with the score at 0–0. They beat Romania, Finland, Armenia and Andorra, home and away, too.

Ruud van Nistelrooy, who led their scorers with seven goals, said: "We're doing well but we're still growing as a team. This is not a team filled with big names, like at Euro 2004, but we have excellent quality. We're unbeaten for 16 matches: we scored more points in qualifying than any other side and we conceded just three goals."

Van Basten can choose from a wealth of attacking talent. So much that the coach warned Mark van Bommel he might miss out unless he became a regular starter at Barcelona.

Chelsea's flying winger Arjen Robben is building a growing reputation, Bayern Munich's Roy Makaay is an ideal deputy for Van Nistelrooy while Ajax's Wesley Sneijder offers another threat from midfield.

Holland are playing the free-flowing, attacking football that has been their trademark since the great days of Cruyff. They scored 27 goals in their 12 qualifying games. But perhaps another statistic should be emphasised.

As Van Nistelrooy said, they conceded only three. Finland, in October 2004, were the last team to score against them in a competitive game. That defensive solidity gives the Dutch sound foundations for another major World Cup assault in Germany.

MEXICO

GOING UP IN THE WORLD

This will be Mexico's 13th appearance in the finals but a doping scandal and managerial controversy meant that reaching Germany was not as simple a task as results from their goal-hungry qualifying campaign might suggest.

Mexico were furious to lose to the United States in the second round of the finals four years ago in Jeonju, South Korea. They believed that the evident weakness of the European challenge, player fatigue, was opening up the knock-out stage for them.

Instead, they were outrun by the Americans, a defeat which rankled because it was at the hands of neighbours whom the Mexicans have traditionally believed inferior when comparing football traditions.

Qualifying for Germany was a comparatively simple process, albeit extended since the "Tri" played their opening tie against Dominica on June 19, 2004 and their concluding joust away to Trinidad and Tobago on October 12, 2005. In between they won all but three of their 18 games, scoring an average of 3.7 goals per game.

WORLD CUP RECORD

1930 1st round	1974 did not qualify
1934 did not qualify	1978 1st round
1938 did not enter	1982 did not qualify
1950 1st round	1986 quarter-finals
1954 1st round	1990 suspended
1958 1st round	1994 2nd round
1962 1st round	1998 2nd round
1966 1st round	2002 2nd round
1970 quarter-finals	

STAR PERFORMERS

Oswaldo Sanchez
↗ Goalkeeper ↗ Chivas Guadalajara
↗ Born: September 21, 1973

Pavel Pardo
↗ Midfielder ↗ America
↗ Born: July 26, 1976

Jaime Lozano
↗ Centre forward ↗ UNAM
↗ Born: September 29, 1979

Jared Borgetti
↗ Centre forward ↗ Bolton Wanderers
↗ Born: August 14, 1973

Jose Francisco Fonseca
↗ Forward ↗ Cruz Azul ↗ Born: October 2, 1979

Mexico also competed in the regional championship, the Gold Cup, in the spring of 2005, reaching only the quarter-finals. That result created immediate problems for Ricardo La Volpe, the Argentine coach who had been appointed national manager in the autumn of 2002.

La Volpe – like his US counterpart Bruce Arena, a former goalkeeper – had played, settled and then coached in Mexico. He was hardly a foreigner. But he came under particularly fierce criticism from Hugo Sanchez, the highly popular former Mexico top scorer and now a successful club coach. Indeed, at one stage it appeared only a matter of time before Sanchez was appointed in La Volpe's place.

THE ROAD TO THE FINALS

1st stage	
W 10-0	away v Dominica (Bautista 2, Borgetti 2, Marquez, Osorno, Lozano 2, Davino, Palencia)
W 8-0	home v Dominica (Bautista 2, Borgetti 2, Lozano 2, Oteo, Altamirano)
	Mexico 18-0 on agg
2nd stage	
W 3-1	away v Trinidad and Tobago (Arellano 2, Borgetti)
W 7-0	home v St Vincent & Grenadines (Borgetti 4, Lozano 2, Santana)
W 1-0	away v St Vincent & Grenadines (Borgetti)
W 3-0	home v Trinidad and Tobago (Zinha, Lozano 2)
W 5-0	away v St Kitts and Nevis (Altamirano, Fonseca 2, Santana 2)
W 8-0	home v St Kitts and Nevis (Altamirano, Perez 3, Fonseca 2, Osorno, Santana)
Final group	
W 2-1	away v Costa Rica (Lozano 2)
W 2-1	home v United States (Borgetti, Zinha)
D 1-1	away v Panama (Morales)
W 2-0	away v Guatemala (Zinha, Cabrera)
W 2-0	home v Trinidad and Tobago (Borgetti, Perez)
W 2-0	home v Costa Rica (Borgetti, Fonseca)
L 0-2	away v United States
W 5-0	home v Panama (Perez, Marquez, Borgetti, Fonseca, Pardo)
W 5-2	home v Guatemala (Franco, Fonseca 4)
L 1-2	away v Trinidad and Tobago (Lozano)

ABOVE: Goal poacher extraordinaire, Jared Borgetti scored 14 goals in the run-up to the finals. He plays for Bolton Wanderers in the Premiership.

At least Mexico's qualifying progress left no room for complaint and they were happily on course when they interrupted the process again in June 2005 to compete at the Confederations Cup in Germany.

Here the Mexicans beat world champions Brazil 1–0 in the first round through a header from Jared Borgetti and lost only on penalties to Argentina in the semi-finals. In the third-place play-off, they only lost to hosts Germany in another penalty shoot-out.

That outstanding result went virtually unnoticed, however, because of a doping scandal.

Defenders Salvador Carmona and Aaron Galindo were dropped from the squad after the win over Brazil. Initially La Volpe blamed this on curfew-breaching indiscipline which began to look increasingly like a smokescreen.

Later the Mexican federation admitted the two players had tested positive for a prohibited anabolic steroid after federation-organised dope tests just before the squad flew to Germany.

Both players were subsequently suspended worldwide by FIFA for a year and the Mexican federation was fined £350,000 for its chaotic handling of the case which, at one stage, risked their expulsion from the Confederations Cup.

Ironically, the scandal cemented La Volpe's position because replacing him at that stage would have incurred only further controversy and confusion. Assuring fans that "we have an entire squad of fine players and do not depend on two individuals", La Volpe and his men set out to prove the point in the remaining qualifying matches.

Centre-forward Borgetti, who became the first Mexican to play top-flight football in England when he signed for Bolton Wanderers last August, was the Mexicans' top scorer en route to Germany. He scored 14 goals and was ably supported by the consistently dangerous Jaime Lozano (11) and Francisco Fonseca (8).

Mexico's national team, whoever the coach, have always played to a rhythm and tactical style all their own. Outstanding technique and the players' natural delight in expressing their talents mean the ball is circulated freely around the pitch with often what appears to be dangerously thin defensive cover.

Their ability to make the tactic work in both attack and defence has owed much down the years to players such as record international Claudio Suarez (172 caps) and his successor as defensive co-ordinator, Rafael Marquez.

For years Mexico were perpetually vulnerable World Cup competitors. The weak standards in Central and North America meant they qualified easily for each succeeding World Cup but were seldom good enough against top-quality opposition. The only modern finals tournament they missed was 1990 since they had been barred from entering that World Cup as punishment for fielding over-age players in a preceding youth championship.

Now, however, Mexico have attained higher status. Rising standards of competition throughout the CONCACAF region have sharpened their awareness, while the domestic game is financed as generously by television as it is followed passionately by fans.

That, of course, ratchets up the pressure on La Volpe and his players. As Marquez said: "Nowadays we have much higher standards and expectations to meet. The fans all tell us the same thing: if we reach 'only' the second round again then we will have failed. But, in any case, I honestly believe we are better than that."

COACH

Ricardo Antonio La Volpe

↗ Born: February 6, 1952

La Volpe knows all about not only competing at a World Cup but winning it – as reserve goalkeeper in Argentina's squad in 1978. He played his club football with Banfield and San Lorenzo and then with Atlante and Oaxtepec in Mexico before staying on as a coach. Later he coached Atlante to the Mexican league title before taking over as national coach after Javier Aguirre resigned following the 2002 World Cup finals.

STAR PLAYER

Rafael Marquez

↗ Central defender ↗ Barcelona

↗ Born: February 13, 1979

Marquez is both Mexico's captain and key player. The team's positive style means they depend heavily on a central defender who is adept at anticipating danger and effective in the tackle. Those qualities earned Marquez his debut at 17 with Atlas of Guadalajara, then a move to Europe with Monaco. He won the French league in his first season, starred in Mexico's run to the second round of the 2002 World Cup then joined Barcelona for £3.5million a year later. Injuries meant a switch to defensive midfield in his first season when they finished second in the league but he reverted to his favourite role to anchor their 2005 Liga success.

IRAN

THIRD TIME LUCKY?

World Cup experience and German-based stars hold the key for Iran. Boss Branko Ivankovic wants them to progress beyond the first round for the first time in their history and upset some of the traditional global superpowers along the way.

Iran are one of the traditional powers of the Asian game and are making their third appearance in the finals and second in three tournaments.

First time out they surprised Scotland by snatching a 1–1 draw in Argentina in 1978 but they have yet to progress beyond the first round despite a high-profile victory over the United States in France in 1998, their only victory so far in the finals.

In 2002 Iran missed out on a place at the party in Korea and Japan after losing a dramatic two-leg intercontinental play-off against the Republic of Ireland.

This time, however, they determined right from the outset to avoid being forced to depend on a play-off lottery to reach Germany and things ran remarkably to plan. They lost only twice in 12 qualifying ties and one of those defeats was right at the end of the series, against group-winners Japan, when only pride was at stake.

COACH

Branko Ivankovic

↗ Born: February 28, 1954 (Croatia)
↗ Appointed: October 2003
↗ Previous: Varteks, Segesta, Rijeka (all Croatia)

THE ROAD TO THE FINALS

1st round	
Bye	
2nd round, group one	
W 3-1	home v Qatar (Vahedi, Mahdavikia, Daei)
W 7-0	away v Laos (Daei 2, Enayati 2, Khouphachansy, Taghipour 2)
L 0-1	home v Jordan
W 2-0	away v Jordan (Vahedi, Daei)
W 3-2	away v Qatar (Hashemian 2, Borhani)
W 7-0	home v Laos (Daei 4, Nekounam 2, Borhani)
3rd round, group B	
D 0-0	away v Bahrain
W 2-1	home v Japan (Hashemian 2)
W 2-0	away v North Korea (Mahdavikia, Nekounam)
W 1-0	home v North Korea (Rezaei)
W 1-0	home v Bahrain (Nosrati)
L 1-2	away v Japan (Daei)

STAR PLAYER

Ali Daei

↗ Striker ↗ Saba Battery
↗ Born: March 21, 1969

Daei is a veteran of Iran's squad from the 1998 World Cup in France and has since become the world's all-time leading international marksman with more than 100 goals for his country.

WORLD CUP RECORD

1930-70 did not enter	1990 did not qualify
1974 did not qualify	1994 did not qualify
1978 1st round	1998 1st round
1982 did not enter	2002 did not qualify
1986 disqualified	

STAR PERFORMERS

Javad Nekounam
↗ Midfield ↗ Pas ↗ Born: December 12, 1980

Ali Karimi
↗ Midfield ↗ Bayern Munich
↗ Born: November 8, 1978

Mehdi Mahdavikia
↗ Midfield ↗ Hamburg ↗ Born: July 24, 1977

Fereydoon Zandi
↗ Midfield ↗ Kaiserslautern
↗ Born: April 26, 1979

Vahid Hashemian
↗ Forward ↗ Hannover ↗ Born: July 21, 1976

Veteran striker Ali Daei was leading scorer in the Asian qualifying section with nine goals, including four in the 7–0 win over Laos with which the Iranians secured their place in the final group series.

Iran have been Asian champions three times and won gold at the Asian Games on four occasions. The national coach who steered them to Germany is a Croat, Branko Ivankovic. He took over in the autumn of 2002 and has built a hard-working, disciplined team around a mixture of new youngsters plus a handful of seasoned veterans who are already in Germany with Bundesliga clubs.

Veterans from 1998 such as Daei and playmaker Mehdi Mahdavikia are among them as well as new hero Ali Karimi, who was voted Asian Footballer of the Year in 2004 after finishing joint top scorer at the Asian Cup.

Using tried and tested methods, Iran tend to work very hard to put pressure on the opposition.

Ivankovic is realistic about the task ahead. He is not dreaming of winning the World Cup or even emulating the achievement of fellow Asian representatives South Korea from 2002 in reaching the last four. But he expects to prove a thorn in the side of the major contenders.

As he says: "We already have a lot of enthusiam and ability which will surprise people – and we can only improve as we prepare for the finals."

ANGOLA

OUT OF THE SHADOWS

Fabrice Akwa and his World Cup newcomers give the people of Angola something to cheer after the tragedy of so many war-torn years. The new heroes are stepping up as the *Palancas Negras* emerge at last from the colonial shadows.

What a difference six minutes makes. That is how long was left of Angola's final qualifying game, away to Rwanda, when Fabrice 'Akwa' Maieco struck the goal that will long be feted in the southern African nation.

It both eliminated Nigeria and made sure war-ravaged Angola booked their maiden place in the World Cup finals, prompting understandable delirium in the streets back home. A 28-year civil war killed around one million people and destroyed much of the country's infrastructure. But, at last, the country had something to celebrate.

The seeds of success can be traced back to 2001 when coach Luis Oliveira Goncalves led the Under-20s to victory at the African Youth Championship and then to the last 16 at the FIFA World Youth Championship in Argentina.

When Goncalves took over the *Palancas Negras* (the Black Sables) in late 2003, he drew from that same wellspring of talent, but even he did not expect such remarkable results.

He says: "Being drawn in the same group as Nigeria, Zimbabwe, Rwanda, Gabon and Algeria meant it was never going to be easy. But when we found we were leading the group at halfway we realised we could do it. Our self-belief soared even more after we took a point off Nigeria away from home."

Yet Angola almost fell in the preliminary qualifying rounds, They lost 3–1 to Chad in the first leg, only for Qatar-based striker Fabrice Akwa and Belenenses' Bruno Mauro to secure a 2–0 second-leg victory that saw them advance on away goals.

Angola achieved independence from Portugal as little as 30 years ago. They first entered the World Cup in 1986 and home-based members of the current squad are semi-professional. Anything they achieve in Germany will be a bonus.

"What you'll see will be tactical discipline, rigour and application," says Goncalves. "Those of us who have qualified for the World Cup for the first time have achieved it by getting organised and improving our game."

Old heroes included Jose Aguas and Joaquim Santana who won the European Cup with Benfica in the early 1960s and played all of their national team football for Portugal. Angola-born coach Carlos Queiroz later turned Portugal into world youth champions. Now the country has a new generation of heroes of their own.

WORLD CUP RECORD

1930-74 did not exist	1990 did not qualify
1978 not eligible	1994 did not qualify
1982 did not enter	1998 did not qualify
1986 did not qualify	2002 did not qualify

STAR PERFORMERS

Joao Pereira
↗ Goalkeeper ↗ Moreirense
↗ Born: January 7, 1970

Andre
↗ Midfielder ↗ Kuwait SC
↗ Born: May 14, 1978

Gilberto
↗ Midfield/forward ↗ Al Ahly (Egypt)
↗ Born: September 21, 1982

Bruno Mauro
↗ Forward ↗ Belenenses
↗ Born: April 17, 198

Fabrice Maieco 'Akwa'
↗ Midfield ↗ Qatar SC
↗ Born: December 12, 1976

COACH

Luis Oliveira Goncalves
↗ Born: March 4, 1964 (in Portugal)
↗ Appointed: October 2003
↗ Previous: Angola Under-20s

THE ROAD TO THE FINALS

1st round	
L 1-3	away v Chad (Bruno Mauro)
W 2-0	home v Chad (Akwa, Bruno Mauro)
Angola on away goals, agg 3-3	
2nd round	
D 0-0	away v Algeria
W 1-0	home v Nigeria (Akwa)
D 2-2	away v Gabon (Akwa, Marco Paulo)
W 1-0	home v Rwanda (Freddy)
W 1-0	home v Zimbabwe (Flavio)
L 0-2	away v Zimbabwe
W 2-1	home v Algeria (Flavio, Akwa)
D 1-1	away v Nigeria (Figueiredo)
W 3-0	home v Gabon (Nsi-Akoue, Mantorras, Ze Kalanga)
W 1-0	away v Rwanda (Akwa)

STAR PLAYER

Pedro Mantorras
↗ Forward ↗ Benfica
↗ Born: March 18, 1982
Mantorras's "arrival" as a teenager earned comparisons with Benfica's Angola-born European Cup-winning stars of the early 1960s. Intends to make amends in Germany for lost time after career-threatening knee trouble.

PORTUGAL

HUNGRY FOR SUCCESS

Pauleta seeks to far surpass Eusebio's goalscoring record, as Portugal bid to revive the glories of 1966 under "Big Phil" Scolari, the former Brazil manager who knows all about the secrets of achieving success at the World Cup finals.

The so-called golden generation failed narrowly to clinch the top prize on home soil at Euro 2004, so what chance do the current crop of Portuguese players have in Germany?

That is the question all their fans will be asking as Luiz Felipe Scolari's side – the so-called Brazilians of Europe who so often flatter to deceive – launch yet another attempt to win one of the two major competitions.

For Scolari, memories of Korea and Japan, when he was in victorious charge of his native Brazil, are bound to come flooding back. Despite a bad press going into the tournament after an up-and-down qualification, Scolari led Brazil to a fifth world title, winning all seven matches in the process.

"Big Phil" stepped down immediately afterwards and launched himself on the Portuguese adventure fortified with the knowledge that he had achieved what his critics had thought impossible – he had won the biggest prize of all.

Portugal, runners-up as hosts to Greece at Euro 2004, secured their place in the 2006 finals with relative ease despite a lacklustre display in the penultimate 2–1 victory over Liechtenstein which punched their ticket. Scolari will thus need to accentuate the positive to get the best out of a squad which boasts some of the most gifted performers in the game in playmaker Deco, attacking midfielder Maniche, outstanding winger Cristiano Ronaldo and veteran Luis Figo.

No-one, however, may be as important to Portugal's cause as Pedro Pauleta. If strikers win tournaments let alone games, the Paris Saint-Germain marksman, who broke Eusebio's all-time Portuguese goalscoring record last autumn, could offer the difference between an outstanding World Cup and yet another disappointing exit.

Pauleta was just one strike behind the legendary Eusebio's tally of 41 going into the final qualifier against Latvia. On 18 minutes he equalled the record, then wrote himself into the history books by claiming it outright two minutes later. Portugal were already through as Group Three winners, but it was still a moment for the country to savour. "I am a little sad that some have not given much importance to my accomplishment," said the Azores-born striker after overtaking Eusebio. "For many people, it seems a crime to surpass Eusebio as the top scorer for Portugal. I can only say that Eusebio is Eusebio and nobody will ever surpass him."

The 32-year-old, who has averaged almost a goal a game throughout his career, found the net in Portugal's first five group matches and now has the chance to take his predatory skills on to the biggest stage of all.

Pauleta may not be as easy on the eye as some of his celebrated team-mates but, according to Benfica's Nuno Gomes who is his main rival for the central striker's role, he has that happy knack of being "always in the right place at the right time".

Gomes says: "He is a typical striker. He plays in the middle of the defenders and is the one who applies the final touch. We're different players – I like to have the ball and get involved in the team play but he is the man to finish the moves off."

On their day, Portugal have shown time after time that they are a match for anyone. But, considering their footballing tradition, which features household names such as Eusebio, Paulo Futre and Figo, it is surprising that they have only taken part in three World Cup finals.

ABOVE: Master of the stepover, Ronaldo is capable of stretching the world's best defenders.

WORLD CUP RECORD

1930 did not enter	1974 did not qualify
1934 did not qualify	1978 did not qualify
1938 did not qualify	1982 did not qualify
1950 did not qualify	1986 1st round
1954 did not qualify	1990 did not qualify
1958 did not qualify	1994 did not qualify
1962 did not qualify	1998 did not qualify
1966 third place	2002 1st round
1970 did not qualify	

STAR PERFORMERS

Paulo Ferreira
↗ Right-back ↗ Chelsea
↗ Born: January 18, 1979

Ricardo Carvalho
↗ Central defender ↗ Chelsea
↗ Born: May 18, 1978

Cristiano Ronaldo
↗ Winger ↗ Manchester United
↗ Born: February 5, 1985

Pauleta (Full name Pedro Resende)
↗ Centre-forward ↗ Paris Saint-Germain
↗ Born: April 28, 1973

Simao Sabrosa
↗ Winger ↗ Benfica ↗ Born: October 30, 1978

COACH

Luiz Felipe Scolari

↗ Born: November 9, 1948

Scolari took over Portugal at the start of 2003, six months after guiding Brazil to a fifth World Cup. Never a top-rank player, he scored managerial success in the South American club cup with Gremio and Palmeiras and also worked successfully in the Middle East, Egypt and Japan. Never made a secret of sometimes encouraging his players to "kill" a game.

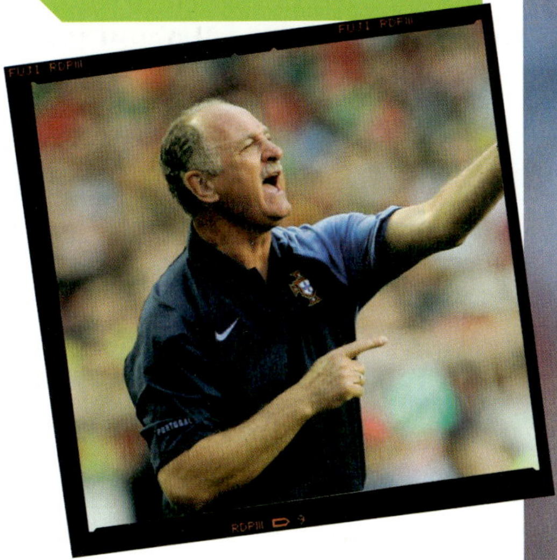

STAR PLAYER

Luis Figo

↗ Forward ↗ Internazionale

↗ Born: November 4, 1972

Figo is playing his last World Cup after coming back into contention midway through the qualifying campaign after initially retiring from international football following his upset at Portugal's defeat by Greece in the final of Euro 2004. Figo made his name as a versatile forward with Sporting and then became possibly the finest right winger in Europe with Barcelona after a transfer to Italy fell through. In summer 2000 he moved to Real Madrid, earning hate status back in Barcelona but adding the Champions League to his trophies in 2002. Honours have included election as European Footballer of the Year and FIFA World Player of the Year.

THE ROAD TO THE FINALS

W 2-0	away v Latvia (Ronaldo, Pauleta)
W 4-0	home v Estonia (Ronaldo, Postiga 2, Pauleta)
D 2-2	away v Liechtenstein (Pauleta, Hasler og)
W 7-1	home v Russia (Pauleta, Ronaldo 2, Deco, Simao, Petit 2)
W 5-0	away v Luxembourg (Federspiel og, Ronaldo, Maniche, Pauleta 2)
D 1-1	away v Slovakia (Helder)
W 2-0	home v Slovakia (Meira, Ronaldo)
W 1-0	away v Estonia (Ronaldo)
W 6-0	home v Luxembourg (Andrade, Carvalho, Pauleta 2, Simao 2)
D 0-0	away v Russia
W 2-1	home v Liechtenstein (Pauleta, Nuno Gomes)
W 3-0	home v Latvia (Pauleta 2, Viana)

Their debut appearance was a memorable one as Eusebio, the "Black Panther", led his side to a surprise third place in England in 1966. His top-scoring tally including a sensational four which propelled his team past North Korea from 3–0 down for a remarkable 5–3 quarter-final victory.

In all, he scored nine times to finish top marksman in the tournament, but it would be another 20 years before Portugal reappeared in the world spotlight, heading for home after the first round at Mexico in 1986 despite beating England.

A disastrous exit in the first round in Korea and Japan has made them all the more hungry for success in Germany – especially Pauleta, whose first hat-trick for his country in the 4–0 defeat of Poland in 2002 was a special, if ultimately unrewarding, moment.

Another household name desperate to show up at his best is Internazionale's Figo, Portugal's most-capped player who is now 33 and will retire permanently from international football after the finals.

Shortly after Portugal finished runners-up to Greece at Euro 2004, Figo decided on an indefinite break from the international stage. But in May the following year, he agreed to a recall for World Cup qualifiers against Slovakia and Estonia. Now he intends to make the most of his second chance.

ITALY

REBIRTH OF THE BLUES

Italy were the first European nation to win the World Cup three times. That just means extra pressure on the Serie A superstars. So coach Marcello Lippi is hoping his softy, softly approach can pay off for the *Azzurri* in Germany.

Coach Marcello Lippi has been trying as hard as he can to play down the hype ever since Italy began closing in on the World Cup finals.

Italy are always one of the favourites. Only once, in 1958, have they failed to qualify. They won the World Cup in 1934, 1938 and 1982. They reached the final in 1970 and 1994, losing to Brazil in both. They finished third on home soil in 1990.

But their last two campaigns have been less successful. They lost to France on penalties in the 1998 quarter-finals and four years later, they were eliminated controversially on a golden goal by co-hosts South Korea.

Lippi's *Azzurri* qualified for Germany by topping European Group Five, an appropriate five points ahead of Norway. They lost just once but five of their seven wins came by a single goal as Lippi searched long and hard for his best attacking combination.

Italy's last group games – both at home – showed the problem. Substitute Cristian Zaccardo scored the only goal in a 1–0 win over Slovenia that clinched their place in Germany then Alberto Gilardino netted just five minutes from time to secure a 2–1 victory over Moldova.

Lippi hid his concerns, preferring to praise the players' resilience. He says: "It's vital to have the right mentality. Above all, I'm very satisfied with the team spirit and the way the players have worked together. That's the basis for success."

Lippi, who steered Juventus to three Champions League finals, had succeeded Giovanni Trapattoni after Italy failed to advance beyond the group stage at Euro 2004.

His first match ended in a shock 2–0 friendly defeat by Iceland but a 1–0 qualifying reverse in Slovenia was the only defeat in Lippi's next 15 matches. He used 63 players in his first 18 months in charge but claims to have whittled them down to 30 candidates for the finals. He says: "The first year was about testing things out. I found some valid options and some less so. After that I reduced things."

Lippi's low-key preparation contrasts with Trapattoni's bullish approach before the 2002 finals. He

WORLD CUP RECORD

1930 did not enter	1974 1st round
1934 champions	1978 fourth place
1938 champions	1982 champions
1950 1st round	1986 2nd round
1954 1st round	1990 third place
1958 did not qualify	1994 runners-up
1962 1st round	1998 quarter-finals
1966 1st round	2002 2nd round
1970 runners-up	

STAR PERFORMERS

Fabio Cannavaro
↗ Central defender ↗ Internazionale
↗ Born: September 13, 1973

Andrea Pirlo
↗ Midfielder ↗ AC Milan
↗ Born: May 19, 1979

Francesco Totti
↗ Forward ↗ Roma
↗ Born: September 27, 1976

Alessandro Del Piero
↗ Forward ↗ Juventus
↗ Born: November 9, 1974

Alberto Gilardino
↗ Striker ↗ AC Milan ↗ Born: July 5, 1982

LEFT: AC Milan's Andrea Pirlo is Italy's playmaker as well as being their foremost dead-ball specialist.

THE ROAD TO THE FINALS

W 2-1	home v Norway (De Rossi, Toni)
W 1-0	away v Moldova (Del Piero)
L 0-1	away v Slovenia
W 4-3	home v Belarus (Totti 2, De Rossi, Gilardino)
W 2-0	home v Scotland (Pirlo 2)
D 0-0	away v Norway
D 1-1	away v Scotland (Grosso)
W 4-1	away v Belarus (Toni 3, Camoranesi)
W 1-0	home v Slovenia (Zaccardo)
W 2-1	home v Moldova (Vieri, Gilardino)

says: "Everyone knows Brazil are the favourites. But I was happy to hear Ronaldo say that behind the Brazilians are four or five teams who could be a threat and Italy are in that category."

The *Azzurri* defence will be as hard to penetrate as ever. Juventus goalkeeper Gigi Buffon remains one of the world's best after recovering from a shoulder injury and clubmate Fabio Cannavaro and Milan's Alessandro Nesta form a formidable central defensive partnership.

Lippi believes he may have solved Italy's full-back problem, following the international retirement of Paolo Maldini, by switching Juventus's Gianluca Zambrotta to the right and introducing Palermo's Fabio Grosso on the left.

Midfield has a settled look. Milan's Gennaro Gattuso is the ball-winner and anchor. Club colleague Andrea Pirlo is the playmaker, while Camoranesi of Juventus bustles from box to box. Roma's Francesco Totti can make amends for two disastrous tournaments as he plays in support of two strikers. But which two? The *Azzurris'* fate may depend on Lippi's answer.

Milan's Alberto Gilardino is Italy's new hope, but failed to establish himself during the qualifiers. Luca Toni, of Fiorentina, netted three against Belarus but scored only one other goal in the qualifiers while Udinese's Vincenzo Iaquinta lacks national team experience.

Christian Vieri, of Milan, and Alex Del Piero of Juventus are experienced but injury-prone, while Antonio Cassano's World Cup dreams were shaken by a contract squabble which cost him his place last autumn at Roma.

Another complication may be the mere process of advancing through the early stages. Italy were eliminated at the group stage on German soil 32 years ago after losing to Poland in Stuttgart.

Even when they won the World Cup in 1982, they had teething troubles before beating Diego Maradona's Argentina and Brazil in the second phase. Of course then they outclassed Poland in the semi-finals and West Germany 3–1 in the final.

Paolo Rossi finished as tournament top scorer with six goals. Yet he and the rest of manager Enzo Bearzot's squad felt the full wrath of the media after their initial group draws against Poland, Peru and Cameroon.

Looking back, Cup-winning skipper and goalkeeper Dino Zoff says: "We could only relax a little once we'd qualified for the second phase. We felt so much pressure on us in the early stages because we had been built up as one of the favourites. We were expected to qualify easily. When we didn't, the media attacked us. That's how it always is for Italy."

Which is why Lippi is so wary of talking up his team's chances.

COACH

Marcello Lippi

↗ Born: April 12, 1948

Lippi brought a winner's pedigree to the job of national coach after guiding Juventus to five Serie A titles and further success in the World Club Cup, Champions League (one win in four finals) and European Supercup. He was the obvious candidate when Giovanni Trapattoni, a playing contemporary and another former defender, stepped down after Euro 2004.

STAR PLAYER

Gianluigi Buffon

↗ Goalkeeper ↗ Juventus

↗ Born: January 28, 1978

Even before he left Parma in 2001 to join Juventus for a world goalkeeping record fee of £24million, Buffon ranked among the finest goalkeepers in the world. He lives up to that reputation at both international and domestic level, having conceded less than a goal a game in 11 years in Serie A and winning the UEFA Cup, three Italian leagues titles, the Italian cup and three Italian Supercups along the way. He made the first of around 60 Italy appearances in a 1–1 draw against Russia in October 1997. Missed the first half of this 2005–06 season after suffering a shoulder fracture in Juventus' defeat by Internazionale in the pre-season Italian Supercup.

GHANA

RISING STARS

Ghana are long overdue an appearance on the big stage after their successes in Africa and at world junior level. Now Michael Essien must drive them forward – just as he did in their runaway triumph in the qualifying campaign.

Ghana carry Africa's highest hopes into the 2006 World Cup. Remarkably, though the Black Stars boast four African Nations Cups and two world Under-17 titles, this is their first appearance in the World Cup finals.

It has been a long road for Ghana, who first competed in the qualifying competition in 1960–61 – the same year they scored a famous 4–3 victory over the legendary Real Madrid of Alfredo Di Stefano and Ferenc Puskas.

But the west African nation probably now has its best-ever team – inspired by the midfield trio of Fenerbahce's Stephen Appiah, Chelsea's record signing Michael Essien and Udinese's Sulley Muntari.

They also have strength in depth and have been more or less on a continuous roll since the arrival of coach Ratomir Dujkovic in December 2004.

Previously, the Croat's Rwanda team had wrecked Ghana's qualifying bid for the 2004 African Nations finals. He soon caused outrage and controversy by squabbling with captain Samuel Kuffour after the Roma defender failed to turn up at a training camp.

Dujkovic asserted his authority by dropping Kuffour temporarily from the squad. His authoritarian approach appeared to galvanise a team who had lost their opening match in Burkina Faso. They went unbeaten through the rest of the campaign to finish five points ahead of Democratic Republic of Congo.

The key game for Dujkovic's team was a 2–0 win over South Africa in Johannesburg with goals from Essien and Matthew Amoah.

Dujkovic's thoughtful preparation – a week's training at similar altitude in Kenya – showed his attention to detail. Ghana then finished with a flourish, winning 2–0 against Uganda and 4–0 in the Cape Verde Islands.

The team from the former Gold Coast is based on a rock-solid defence which conceded just four goals in 10 qualifying games. But the Black Stars do not always score the goals their approach play threatens. Ghana lack the flair strikers of bygone days, such as Abedi Pele and Anthony Yeboah. Appiah and Gyan Asamoah were joint top scorers with four goals apiece followed by three each for Essien and Amoah, who was recalled, profitably, after a two-year absence. The lesson is that the Black Stars will need plenty of goals from midfield to progress in Germany.

STAR PERFORMERS

Samuel Kuffour
↗ Central defender ↗ Roma
↗ Born: September 3, 1976

Stephen Appiah
↗ Midfielder ↗ Fenerbahce
↗ Born: December 24, 1980

Sulley Ali Muntari
↗ Midfielder ↗ Udinese
↗ Born: August 27, 1984

Gyan Asamoah
↗ Forward ↗ Modena
↗ Born: November 22, 1985

Matthew Amoah
↗ Forward ↗ Vitesse Arnhem
↗ Born: October 24, 1980

COACH

Ratomir Dujkovic
↗ Born: February 24, 1946
↗ Appointed December 2004
↗ Previous: Yugoslavia Yth, Venezuela, Myanmar, Rwanda

STAR PLAYER

Michael Essien
↗ Midfielder ↗ Chelsea
↗ Born: December 8, 1982

Essien cost Chelsea £24.4m last year from Lyon with whom his dynamic midfield play had earned two French league titles. Bastia had earlier spotted his teenage talent while with Liberty Professionals back home.

WORLD CUP RECORD

1930-54 did not exist	1982 did not enter
1958 not eligible	1986 did not qualify
1962 did not qualify	1990 did not qualify
1966 did not enter	1994 did not qualify
1970 did not enter	1998 did not qualify
1974 did not qualify	2002 did not qualify
1978 did not qualify	

THE ROAD TO THE FINALS

1st round	
W 5-0	away v Somalia (Arhin Duah 2, Boakye 2, Gyan)
W 2-0	home v Somalia (Appiah, Adjei)
Ghana 7-0 on agg	
2nd round	
L 0-1	away v Burkina Faso
W 3-0	home v South Africa (Muntari, Appiah 2)
D 1-1	away v Uganda (Gyan)
W 2-0	home v Cape Verde (Essien, Veiga og)
D 0-0	home v DR Congo
D 1-1	away v DR Congo (Gyan)
W 2-1	home v Burkina Faso (Appiah, Amoah)
W 2-0	away v South Africa (Amoah, Essien)
W 2-0	home v Uganda (Essien, Amoah)
W 4-0	away v Cape Verde (Asamoah, Muntari, Gyan, Attram)

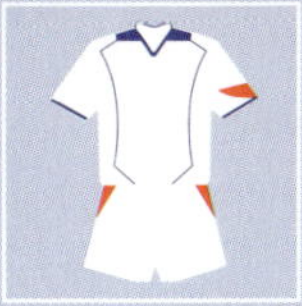

THE USA

THE QUEST FOR WORLD DOMINATION

The Americans are coming . . . and no longer are they ranked among the World Cup minnows. Landon Donovan and his team-mates see 2006 as another step closer to establishing the US as a global soccer superpower.

When Alan Rothenberg, president of the United States federation, welcomed the world to "their" finals in 1994, he promised, with a twinkle in his eye: "Our next target is to win the World Cup in 2010."

Just as that target date is coming closer, so too are the United States. In 1994 they reached the second round as hosts; in 2002 they progressed to the quarter-finals in South Korea and Japan. No longer are the Americans the team of no-hopers whose victory over England in 1950 was considered one of the great World Cup jokes.

As expected, the Americans reached Germany fairly comfortably after the many matches, which constitute the tortuous Caribbean, Central and North American (CONCACAF) qualifying system. They won 11 of their 17 games, scoring 35 goals and conceding a mere 11 with nine clean sheets. No-one stretched them when it mattered, with the predictable exception of the region's traditional giants Mexico and, perhaps surprisingly, Costa Rica who inflicted the Americans' only defeats.

In the likes of veteran keeper Kasey Keller and defenders Eddie Pope and Carlos Bocanegra, the Americans boast the solid foundation of a team who have evolved impressively under the watchful guidance of Bruce Arena – one of the few goalkeepers to hit the heights as a coach.

In addition to the pace of Beasley and the incisive talents of Donovan, the Americans have strengthened attack with the emergence of Ed Johnson, who hit a hat-trick in the 6–0 thrashing of Panama.

Those goals all helped ensure a fifth consecutive appearance at the finals, which keeps the US in impressive step with the elite teams such as Argentina, Brazil and Germany. Their decisive victories along the road to Germany also had the effect of lifting them as high as seventh in the official FIFA world rankings.

Reaching the quarter-finals in Korea and Japan in 2002 was a significant benchmark. As Arena says: "We have come a very long way since France in 1998 and all the euphoria was justified after we got to the quarter-finals in 2002. There remains a lot of work to do, but that performance generated an air of confidence around the team which has stood us in good stead ever since."

STAR PLAYER

Landon Donovan

↗ Forward ↗ Los Angeles Galaxy

↗ Born: March 4, 1982

As a youngster, he was signed by Bayer Leverkusen. But German football did not suit him and he returned home with San Jose and then Galaxy. Donovan, three times Footballer of the Year, marked his senior US debut with a goal against Mexico in October 2000.

WORLD CUP RECORD

1930 semi-finals	1974 did not qualify
1934 1st round	1978 did not qualify
1938 did not enter	1982 did not qualify
1950 1st round	1986 did not qualify
1954 did not qualify	1990 1st round
1958 did not qualify	1994 2nd round
1962 did not qualify	1998 1st round
1966 did not qualify	2002 quarter-finals
1970 did not qualify	

STAR PERFORMERS

Kasey Keller
↗ Goalkeeper ↗ Borussia Monchengladbach
↗ Born: November 29, 1969

Carlos Bocanegra
↗ Fullback ↗ Fulham
↗ Born: May 25, 1979

DeMarcus Beasley
↗ Winger ↗ PSV Eindhoven
↗ Born: May 24, 1982

Brian McBride
↗ Forward ↗ Fulham
↗ Born: June 19, 1972

Ed Johnson
↗ Striker ↗ FC Dallas ↗ Born: March 31, 1984

THE ROAD TO THE FINALS

1st stage	
W 3-0	home v Grenada (Beasley 2, Vanney)
W 3-2	away v Grenada (Donovan, Wolff, Beasley)
	US 6-2 on agg
2nd stage	
D 1-1	away v Jamaica (Ching)
W 2-0	home v El Salvador (Ching, Donovan)
D 1-1	away v Panama (Jones)
W 2-0	away v El Salvador (McBride, Johnson)
W 6-0	home v Panama (Donvan 2, Johnson 3, Torres)
D 1-1	home v Jamaica (Johnson)
Final group	
W 2-1	away v Trinidad and Tobago (Johnson, Lewis)
L 2-1	away v Mexico (Lewis)
W 2-0	home v Guatemala (Johnson, Ralston)
W 3-0	home v Costa Rica (Donovan 2, McBride)
W 3-0	away v Panama (Bocanegra, Donovan, McBride)
W 2-0	home v Mexico (Ralston, Beasley)
D 0-0	away v Guatemala
L 0-3	away v Costa Rica
W 2-0	home v Panama (Martino, Twellman)

COACH

Bruce Arena
↗ Born: September 21, 1951
↗ Appointed: October 1998
↗ Previous: DC United

THE CZECH REPUBLIC

EUROPE'S DARK HORSES

Pavel Nedved comes out of international retirement to help Karel Bruckner's boys try to make amends for the upset in Portugal. Jan Koller's race to regain fitness could be crucial in the bid to pull off another impressive World Cup performance.

The Czech Republic are not only heading into the World Cup finals for the first time in their modern independent right, but will also be the "dark horses" of the event according to Brazil coach Carlos Alberto Parreira.

The Czechs have a proud World Cup history – as Czechoslovakia, they reached the final in both 1934 and 1962. But the country split in 1993, since which time the Czech Republic has prospered, while its counterpart Slovakia has struggled.

The Czechs reached the final of Euro 96 and were unlucky semi-final losers to Greece at Euro 2004 after some excellent displays. They lost to Belgium in the 2002 World Cup play-offs.

This time, they beat Norway 1–0 both home and away in the play-offs. Vladimir Smicer scored the only goal in Oslo and Tomas Rosicky defied an ankle injury to hit the winner in Prague.

That success lifted the Czechs to second place in the FIFA world rankings, second behind World Cup holders Brazil. Coach Karel Bruckner knows they will never have a better chance to make their mark in the finals. But he is sweating on two issues which are beyond his control: the recovery time of injured record scorer Jan Koller, the Republic's giant striker, as well as the willingness of former European Footballer of the Year Pavel Nedved to continue his return from international retirement.

The Czechs beat Norway with Nedved back in the side after a 16-month absence, but minus cruciate ligament victim Koller.

Norway coach Age Hareide said: "They were just too good for us in both games. They'll do very well in the finals. They're probably capable of winning the tournament. They have an outstanding midfield and a world-class goalkeeper in Petr Cech."

Bruckner believes that 33-year-old Nedved, who came back because of an injury crisis, will play in Germany along with other members of the "older generation" such as Karel Poborsky (34), Vladimir Smicer (31) and Tomas Galasek (33).

Bruckner says: "Pavel is a leader. He saw what was happening and took the responsibility on himself. We're a strong team and, with his influence, we're even stronger."

Nedved's influence was obviously missed in the qualifying defeats by Holland and Romania, which left the Czechs trying to play catch-up with the Dutch. Now the Juventus star approaches his one last chance to play in the World Cup finals. He

WORLD CUP RECORD

1930 did not enter	1974 did not qualify
1934 runners-up	1978 did not qualify
1938 quarter-finals	1982 1st round
1950 did not enter	1986 did not qualify
1954 1st round	1990 quarter-finals
1958 1st round	1994 did not qualify
1962 runners-up	1998 did not qualify
1966 did not qualify	2002 did not qualify
1970 1st round	

(known as Czechoslovakia until 1993)

STAR PERFORMERS

Petr Cech
↗ Goalkeeper ↗ Chelsea
↗ Born: May 20, 1982

Marek Jankulovski
↗ Left-back ↗ AC Milan
↗ Born: May 9, 1977

Tomas Rosicky
↗ Midfielder ↗ Borussia Dortmund
↗ Born: October 4, 1980

Milan Baros
↗ Centre-forward ↗ Aston Villa
↗ Born: October 28, 1981

Jan Koller
↗ Centre-forward ↗ Borussia Dortmund
↗ Born: March 30, 1973

THE ROAD TO THE FINALS

L 0-2	home v Holland
W 1-0	home v Romania (Koller)
W 3-0	away v Armenia (Koller 2, Rosicky)
W 2-0	away v Macedonia FR (Lokvenc, Koller)
W 4-3	home v Finland (Baros, Rosicky, Polak, Lokvenc)
W 4-0	away v Andorra (Jankulovski pen, Baros, Lokvenc, Rosicky)
W 8-1	home v Andorra (Lokvenc 2, Koller, Smicer, Galasek, Baros, Rosicky, Polak)
W 6-1	home v Macedonia FR (Koller 4, Rosicky, Baros)
L 0-2	away v Romania
W 4-1	home v Armenia (Heinz, Polak 2, Baros)
L 0-2	home v Holland
W 3-0	away v Finland (Jun, Rosicky, Heinz)
Play-off:	
W 1-0	away v Norway (Smicer)
W 1-0	home v Norway (Rosicky)
Czech Republic 2-0 on agg	

BELOW: Aston Villa's lightning-quick striker Milan Baros won the Golden Boot at Euro 2004.

COACH

Karel Bruckner

↗ Born: November 13, 1939

One of the oldest coaches at the finals but arguably the most intuitively creative. Bruckner played for Sigma Olomouc and Banik Ostrava, then coached Sigma, Drnovice, Brno and Inter Bratislava, before guiding the Czechs to runners-up spot in the European Under-21 finals in 2000. He was an obvious choice to succeed Jozef Chovanec with the seniors two years later.

STAR PLAYER

Pavel Nedved

↗ Midfielder ↗ Juventus

↗ Born: August 30, 1972

Nedved, European Footballer of the Year in 2003, can trace his mainstream career back to 1996 and the European finals in England. But it was not until after his move from Sparta Prague to Lazio of Italy that his creative talent gained international recognition. Under Sven-Goran Eriksson, Nedved won the Italian league and cup and European Cup-Winners' Cup. He also became the midfield fulcrum of a fine Czech team. It was only, significantly, after he had injured a knee that the Czechs were beaten by Greece in the semi-finals of Euro 2004. Nedved quit the national team to concentrate on his Champions League dream but was recalled because of an injury crisis in autumn 2005.

says: "I hope, together with the other players, that we won't be considered as the lost generation."

Poborsky, the only Czech to win more than 100 caps, was loaned out by Sparta Prague to second division Ceske Budejovice earlier this season after criticising then-coach Jaroslav Hrebik. But Bruckner has continued to trust in his vast experience. It was Poborsky's teasing cross which set up Smicer's winner in Oslo.

Bruckner has a deep reservoir of experience he can call on in most areas of the team. Galasek is the midfield anchor, Nedved drives the team forward and Smicer makes stealthy runs from deep.

Rosicky, one of the stars of the "younger generation", is the playmaker with an eye for goal. He scored seven times in the qualifiers. Jan Polak, who netted four, is another attacking midfielder. So is the up-and-coming Jaroslav Plasil, with Jiri Jarosik and David Jarolim also in reserve.

The Czechs field a settled defence in front of Cech with Milan full-back Marek Jankulovski, who has recovered from a broken ankle, Zdenek Grygera, Tomas Ujfalusi and David Rozenahl. But Bruckner's worries are in attack.

Jan Koller, the Czechs' record scorer with 40 goals, needed major surgery after damaging his left knee playing for Borussia Dortmund against Mainz in September. He was warned he could be out for up to eight months, leaving little time to regain match fitness for the finals.

Happily, Milan Baros hopes to have put persistent Achilles tendon trouble behind him, so he can once again display the immense goal hunger which saw him crowned as leading scorer at Euro 2004.

Bruckner has instilled resilience in the Czech squad. Four days after losing to the Dutch, a Czech side without Koller and Nedved won 3–0 in Finland to clinch their play-off place.

Rosicky notes the difference since Bruckner took charge in 2002. He says: "Four years ago, we lacked discipline and players were getting sent off. That doesn't happen any more. This team have character and self-belief."

The Czechs are also determined to make up for Euro 2004 when Nedved limped off just as they were dominating the semi-final against Greece and they lost 1–0 on a silver goal. Marek Heinz says: "We were probably the best side there, but a soft goal put us out."

The "older generation" – including Jan Koller and Pavel Nedved – have an extra incentive, if one is needed. This will be not only only their first but also their last World Cup finals.

BRAZIL

TEAM OF ALL THE TALENTS

Brazil boast a group of the most highly talented forwards in World Cup history. Only one question nags at the holders: can they find a winning balance between defence and attack in pursuit of a record sixth title?

Brazil is the greatest football nation on earth. England may be the home of the organized modern game but for inspirational genius and World Cup glory no-one comes near the samba soccer superstars.

Coach Carlos Alberto Parreira, and a squad top-heavy with some of the finest forwards in the international game, approach Germany fired by a perceived insult delivered by world-governing body FIFA.

They are the first reigning World Cup holders forced to return for the defence of their title after suffering the indignity of the qualification process. Political complications – first under pressure from Oceania, then under pressure from the rest of South America – produced the bitter compromise which forced Brazil to battle through the qualifying marathon.

European clubs were as angry as Brazilian confederation president Ricardo Teixeira and coach Parreira. Brazil's integration into the qualifiers meant 18 tedious and tiring return flights to South America for star performers such as Real Madrid's Ronaldo, Barcelona's Ronaldinho, Bayern Munich's Lucio as well as Milan's Kaka, Cafu and Dida.

The one notable factor is that not one of Brazil's European-based players complained about the travel or ever thought to suggest they might be omitted from games against minnows such as Bolivia or Venezuela. That demonstates the players' overriding loyalty to the Brazilian cause and pride in wearing the famous yellow shirt.

Brazil's pride is reflected by their status as record five-time winners of the World Cup – in 1958, 1962, 1970, 1994 and 2002 – as well as being the only nation to have competed at all 17 finals tournaments, stretching back to the inaugural event in Uruguay in 1930.

Some of the greatest players in World Cup history have thrilled Brazil's passionate *torcida* with glitz, glamour and glory. The roll of honour ripples from Leonidas and Domingos da Guia in the 1930s to Ademir, Zizinho and Jair in the early 1950s then on via winning heroes Pele, Didi, Garrincha, Jairzinho and Tostao to recent champions such as Romario, Bebeto, Ronaldo and Ronaldinho.

Ronaldo was Brazil's inspiration in South Korea and Japan in 2002 when he scored eight goals including two in the 2–0 final victory over Germany in Yokohama. He then transferred from Italy's Internazionale to Spain's Real Madrid, returning to South America to score the opening goal of Brazil's qualifying campaign in a 2–0 defeat of Colombia.

WORLD CUP RECORD

1930 1st round	1974 fourth place
1934 1st round	1978 third place
1938 third place	1982 2nd round
1950 runners-up	1986 quarter-finals
1954 quarter-finals	1990 2nd round
1958 champions	1994 champions
1962 champions	1998 runners-up
1966 1st round	2002 champions
1970 champions	

STAR PERFORMERS

Lucio (Lucimar da Silva Ferreira)
↗ Central defender ↗ Bayern Munich
↗ Born: May 8, 1978

Ronaldo (Ronaldo Luiz Nazario da Lima)
↗ Centre-forward ↗ Real Madrid
↗ Born: September 22, 1976

Robinho (Robson de Souza)
↗ Forward ↗ Real Madrid
↗ Born: January 25, 1984

Adriano (Adriano Ribeiro Leite)
↗ Centre-forward ↗ Internazionale
↗ Born: February 17, 1982

Kaka (Ricardo Izecson dos Santos Leite)
↗ Forward ↗ AC Milan ↗ Born: April 22, 1982

ABOVE: Born in Rio, Adriano currently plays for Inter Milan where he is nicknamed "The Emperor".

THE ROAD TO THE FINALS

W 2-1	away v Colombia (Ronaldo, Kaka)
W 1-0	home v Ecuador (Ronaldinho)
D 1-1	away v Peru (Rivaldo)
D 3-3	home v Uruguay (Kaka, Ronaldo 2)
D 0-0	away v Paraguay
W 3-1	home v Argentina (Ronaldo 3)
D 1-1	away v Chile (Luis Fabiano)
W 3-1	home v Bolivia (Ronaldo, Ronaldinho, Adriano)
W 5-2	away v Venezuela (Kaka 2, Ronaldo 2, Adriano)
D 0-0	home v Colombia
L 0-1	away v Ecuador
W 1-0	home v Peru (Kaka)
D 1-1	away v Uruguay (Emerson)
W 4-1	home v Paraguay (Ronaldinho 2, Ze Roberto, Robinho)
L 1-3	away v Argentina (Roberto Carlos)
W 5-0	home v Chile (Juan, Robinho, Adriano 3)
D 1-1	away v Bolivia (Juninho)
W 3-0	home v Venezuela (Adriano, Ronaldo, Roberto Carlos)

A narrow home win over Ecuador followed, but draws against Peru, Uruguay and Paraguay forced changes. Parreira, recalled in succession to 2002 winning boss Luiz Felipe Scolari, decided that Rivaldo had lost the edge of pace which had made him a key component in both 1998 and 2002. He also experimented with tactical shapes to close down space in midfield while, simultaneously, being blessed with the emergence of two more attacking heroes in Adriano and Robinho.

Adriano made his presence felt in the qualifiers with goals against Bolivia and Venezuela. Robinho, the highly rated Santos starlet, was promoted to a secure role in attack in the summer of 2005 after Ronaldo had to be rested to recover from the build-up of pressures both on and off the pitch. Robinho's dancing genius down either wing earned him a summer transfer to join Ronaldo in Madrid. The Brazilian confederation was so concerned at his departure for Europe that it tried to block his transfer, but all to no avail.

Robinho demonstrated his brilliance to German fans in June 2005 in the Confederations Cup tournament, which served as a dummy run for the World Cup organizers. Brazil took the Cup by defeating Argentina 4–1 in the final and, while Adriano was the event's top scorer with five goals, it was Robinho who mesmerized both opponents and spectators.

Parreira relies on a solid back four with two raiding full-backs, including old favourite Roberto Carlos, and a tight three-man midfield who work to protect defence and close down space in midfield. Once the likes of Emerson have regained possession, they are under instructions to move the ball forward as quickly as possible and unleash the attack of many talents on their hapless opponents.

The only problem for Parreira is finding a role and a place for all his attacking stars. But a team with the likes of Kaka, Robinho, Adriano, Ronaldo and Ronaldinho at their beck and call need fear no-one.

COACH

Carlos Alberto Parreira

↗ Born: February 27, 1943

Parreira was never a star player but built an early reputation as a coaching and physical training specialist. After progressing up the club coaching ladder in Brazil, he worked successfully in the Middle East, reaching the World Cup finals with Kuwait in 1982, the United Arab Emirates in 1990 and Saudi Arabia in 1998. But his major achievements were in guiding Brazil to World Cup glory in both 1994 and 2002.

STAR PLAYER

Ronaldinho (Ronaldo de Assis Moreira)

↗ Forward ↗ Barcelona

↗ Born: March 21, 1980

Ronaldinho first drew admirers while playing indoor football as a teenager in his native Porto Alegre. He turned professional in the outdoor game with Gremio and was top scorer for Brazil at the World Under-17 Cup in Egypt. He made his debut for Brazil's seniors in 1999 and won the Copa America before transferring to Europe with Paris Saint-Germain in 2001. Within a year he was starring in Brazil's 2002 World Cup win, scoring two goals including a notable 35-yard free-kick against England in the quarter-finals. A year later Ronaldinho was sold to Barcelona with whom he was a Spanish league runner-up in 2004 and champion in 2005.

CROATIA

WARRIORS WITH A CHEQUERED PAST

The Croats' return to the finals is a matter for family pride for boss Zlatko Kranjcar and his playmaker son Niko. Rebuilding work is paying off handsomely for one of the World Cup's most successful new nations of the last decade.

ABOVE: A defensive midfielder who can score goals, Niko Kovac inherited Zvonimir Boban's number 10 shirt and has over 50 caps.

Croatia's World Cup pedigree as an independent nation since breaking away from the former Yugoslavia may not be long ago in terms of time, but they have certainly stamped their mark on the competition in those familiar red-and-white chequered shirts.

In their first appearance in the finals eight years ago, they left an indelible impression by ousting European champions Germany in the quarter-finals and then having the audacity to take the lead against host nation France in the semis.

WORLD CUP RECORD

1930-90 did not exist
1994 did not enter
1998 third place
2002 1st round

Only a brace of goals from Lilian Thuram sent the eventual champions through but a third-place finish, clinched by beating Holland, announced to the world that Croatia had come of age – and quickly.

Four years later they qualified again, this time as group-winners, but failed to reach the last 16 after being defeated by Mexico in the opening game. Robert Prosinecki and Davor Suker, two of their most trusted servants, retired from international football, and coach Mirko Jozic was left with no option but to resign.

He was succeeded by Otto Baric, who led the team on an abortive Euro 2004 mission that ended at the group stage before he, too, resigned.

The task of guiding the team towards Germany thus fell to Zlatko Kranjcar, a former international and father of one of Croatia's rising stars in playmaker Niko Kranjcar.

Others poised for a key role in Germany include defenders Igor Tudor and Josip Simunic, Niko Kovac in midfield and the effervescent Dado Prso of Rangers up front.

Prso – who played in the last, crucial qualifier against group eight rivals Sweden despite a troublesome knee – had an eye-catching tournament despite the occasional row with the coach. Darijo Srna will, however, forever be idolised for scoring the crucial 56th-minute penalty that clinched qualification.

At the start of qualifying, those who remembered Croatia's stunning

STAR PERFORMERS

Tomislav Butina
↗ Goalkeeper ↗ Brugge
↗ Born: March 30, 1974

Igor Tudor
↗ Defender ↗ Siena
↗ Born: April 16, 1974

Niko Kovac
↗ Midfielder ↗ Hertha Berlin
↗ Born: October 15, 1971

Ivan Klasnic
↗ Forward ↗ Werder Bremen
↗ Born: January 29, 1980

Bosko Balaban
↗ Striker ↗ Brugge
↗ Born: October 15, 1978

THE ROAD TO THE FINALS

W 3-0	home v Hungary (Prso 2, Gyepes og)
W 1-0	away v Sweden (Srna)
D 2-2	home v Bulgaria (Srna 2)
W 4-0	home v Iceland (N Kovac 2, Simunic, Prso)
W 3-0	home v Malta (Prso 2, Tudor)
W 3-1	away v Bulgaria (Babic, Tudor, Kranjcar)
W 3-1	away v Iceland (Balaban 2, Srna)
D 1-1	away v Malta (Kranjcar)
W 1-0	home v Sweden (Srna)
D 0-0	away v Hungary

run to the semi-finals in 1998 were understandably wary of taking the cagey Eastern European side lightly. Yet there were just as many reasons to consider them a spent force.

After failing at the group hurdle in 2002 – and again at the 2004 European Championship – the obvious assumption was that the former Yugoslav republic was on the wane. After all, the country is made up of just 4.5 million people and Kranjcar had little in the way of top-level coaching experience.

Yet once the campaign got under way with a 3–0 home victory over Hungary and an impressive 1–0 away win over Sweden in Gothenburg, it seemed the Croats could not possibly falter. Then, in typical style, they seemed to grow

STAR PLAYER

Dado Prso

↗ Striker ↗ Rangers

↗ Born: November 5, 1974

Prso was a late starter in international terms. He worked his way up through the ranks of the club game with Zadar, Hajduk Split and second division Pazinka before moving to France with minnows Rouen and San Raphael, then being 'discovered' by Jean Tigana and signing for Monaco. Injury to Fernando Morientes gave Prso a Champions League start against Deportivo de La Coruna and he took full advantage to score four goals in an 8–3 win. From there it was a short step – despite persistent knee problems – to lead Croatia's attack in the finals of the 2004 European Championship and then secure a transfer on to Scotland's Rangers.

COACH

Zlatko Kranjcar

↗ Born: November 15, 1956

Kranjcar was an outstanding forward in the former Yugoslavia, playing a decade with Dinamo Zagreb and winning one league title. He then starred in Austria with Rapid Vienna and St Polten and was captain of the new Croatia before turning to coaching. He guided Dinamo to three league titles before succeeding Otto Baric as national coach in the summer of 2004.

complacent and made life needlessly difficult for themselves, not least in Malta when the old mental frailties resurfaced and the group eight underdogs earned themselves a surprise draw.

So which Croatia will turn up in Germany? Replacing the likes of Zvonimir Boban, Suker and Prosinecki has not been easy, but in Prso, Tudor, Srna, Kovac and the junior Kranjcar, Croatia have the makings of another fine team, even if the wave of fresh patriotism which inspired the 1990s side has ebbed. "After Malta some people forgot everything good we had done during this qualification," said the coach. "They forgot we defeated Sweden and Bulgaria away from home. I have been in Croat football for a long time, so I know the Croat mentality very well and nothing surprises me. Many thought we wouldn't make it at the start of the competition but my players played like true warriors and we deserved it." Kranjcar's side finished the campaign unbeaten and qualified with one match to spare.

While Kranjcar was an unlikely successor to Baric – many had tipped former Slovenia manager Srecko Katanec – the 48-year-old had an ace up his sleeve, given that his son, 20-year-old Niko, is considered the future of Croat football. Baric had been hesitant to give the *Wunderkind* a run-out but father clearly knew best and Niko has provided the missing link in attacking midfield.

Miroslav Blazevic, who famously led Croatia to bronze in 1998, believes both Croatia and Serbia and Montenegro have a great chance to make a name for themselves in Germany. He says: "I have always been saying that we from the former Yugoslavia have the best football talents in Europe. If we only had the financial power like Germany, France or Italy, I don't think they would be anywhere near us.

"Both Croatia and Serbia have done really well in the qualifiers and Zlatko Kranjcar and Ilija Petkovic have teams with at least as much quality as mine in 1998."

AUSTRALIA

HIDDINK'S MAGIC TOUCH

Guus Hiddink has worked his usual World Cup magic to guide the Socceroos back to the finals for the first time in 32 years. But after Mark Viduka, John Aloisi and their team-mates finally beat the play-off jinx, now comes an even bigger challenge.

STAR PLAYER

Mark Viduka

↗ Striker ↗ Middlesbrough
↗ Born: October 9, 1975

Viduka stars now with Middlesbrough after wandering from Melbourne Croatia to Croatia Zagreb and then on to Celtic and Leeds. Top-scored in 2002-03 with 22 goals but then had to be sold to ease Leeds' cash crisis.

Australia have made it to the World Cup finals at last after losing in the play-offs for the previous three tournaments.

Middlesbrough keeper Mark Schwarzer was the ultimate hero of their penalty shoot-out, play-off win over Uruguay in Sydney, after Mark Bresciano's goal wiped out the South Americans' first leg lead.

Coach Guus Hiddink decided to stick with Schwarzer after toying with the idea of sending on spot-kick expert Zeljko "Jack" Kalac. Schwarzer made crucial saves from Dario Rodriguez and Marcelo Zalayeta, before John Aloisi tucked away the kick that sent the Australians to Germany.

Victory was particularly sweet after losing to Uruguay in the play-offs for the 2002 finals in Korea and Japan. Australia also lost play-offs to Argentina in 1993 and Iran four years later.

Schwarzer says: "For every one of us who's been here for three or four campaigns, the feeling is just fantastic."

Middlesbrough striker Mark Viduka adds: "This squad is much stronger than four years ago and everything about the coach has been superb. He's taken South Korea to the World Cup semi-finals and coached at Real Madrid and PSV Eindhoven, so you can't help but pick up confidence from him."

Australia's challenge will be founded on a Premiership base. Schwarzer and Viduka, Blackburn's Lucas Neill and Brett Emerton, Everton midfielder Tim Cahill and Liverpool winger Harry Kewell are all likely starters.

Hiddink, who took over from Frank Farina in June, has changed systems from 4-4-2 to 3-5-2, with Neill, Tony Popovic and Tony Vidmar at the back and Emerton and Kewell on the flanks. He says: "They're an easy group to coach. Qualifying was a huge target after so long, but they were eager to face it."

Hiddink stayed true to his positive image by gambling on Kewell – troubled by injury for months – as a 31st-minute substitute after Popovic was booked in the second leg against Uruguay.

The Australians' aggressive approach was a hallmark of their qualifying campaign. Hiddink is demanding more discipline in the finals.

WORLD CUP RECORD

1930-62 did not enter	1986 did not qualify
1966 did not qualify	1990 did not qualify
1970 did not qualify	1994 did not qualify
1974 1st round	1998 did not qualify
1978 did not qualify	2002 did not qualify
1982 did not qualify	

STAR PERFORMERS

Mark Schwarzer
↗ Goalkeeper ↗ Middlesbrough
↗ Born: October 6, 1972

Brett Emerton
↗ Midfield ↗ Blackburn Rovers
↗ Born: February 22, 1979

Tim Cahill
↗ Midfield ↗ Everton
↗ Born: December 6, 1979

Harry Kewell
↗ Forward ↗ Liverpool
↗ Born: September 22, 1978

John Aloisi
↗ Striker ↗ Alaves
↗ Born: February 5, 1976

THE ROAD TO THE FINALS

2nd round	
W 1-0	home v New Zealand (Bresciano)
W 9-0	home v Tahiti (Cahill, Skoko, Simon, Cahill, Sterjovski 3, Zdrilic, Chipperfield)
W 6-1	home v Fiji (Madaschi 2, Cahill 3, Elrich)
W 3-0	away v Vanuatu (Aloisi 2, Emerton)
D 2-2	away v Solomon Islands (Cahill, Emerton)
3rd round	
W 7-0	home v Solomon Islands (Culina, Viduka 2, Cahill, Chipperfield,Thompson, Emerton)
W 2-1	away v Solomon Islands (Thompson, Emerton)
Play-off	
L 0-1	v Uruguay
W 1-0	v Uruguay (Bresciano)
Australia 4-2 on pens, aggregate 1-1	

COACH

Guus Hiddink

↗ Born: November 8, 1946 ↗ Appointed: June 2005 ↗ Previous: PSV Eindhoven, Fenerbahce (Turkey), Valencia (Spain), Holland, Real Madrid (Spain),

He says: "At times we've given away too many fouls. So I've told the players not to be over-eager when going into tackles. We must try to stop conceding free kicks in dangerous positions."

JAPAN

THE HARD WORK BEGINS

Brazil's old hero Zico is setting the agenda as Japan prepare to go into battle this time without the fanatical support of their home fans. Still, stars such as Hidetoshi Nakata and Shunsuke Nakamura know all about European conditions.

Japanese World Cup ambition was given a kick-start by England's Sir Stanley Rous, then the president of FIFA, back in the mid-1960s. It was Rous who suggested a country with enormous drive, albeit lacking a professional league, might one day host the World Cup.

That dream ultimately fired the launch of the J.League in the mid-1990s and Japan's role as co-hosts of the World Cup in 2002. Appearing at the finals for only the second time, they reached the second round before bowing out against Turkey.

Four years earlier, on their debut in France, the Japanese had flown home after the first round. Now moving one step further on by reaching the quarter-finals is the goal for Zico, greatest icon of the J.League era.

The Brazilian had come out of retirement to play for Kashima Antlers in 1993. He returned to Japan late in 2002 to answer the demand for a charismatic national coach in succession to Philippe Troussier.

Zico struggled at first but Asian Cup success in 2004 and subsequent qualification for Germany has cemented his status. Carefully, he rebuilt the team who reached the second round of the 2002 finals, bringing the sparkle of youthful zest to an experienced nucleus built around keeper Yoshi Kawaguchi and the midfield fulcrum of Junichi Inamoto and Hidetoshi Nakata.

The depths of Japan's determination to prepare as thoroughly as possible was revealed in the time it took to reach a fragile agreement with Celtic over the release of playmaker Shunsuke Nakamura for warm-up internationals.

Nakamura's emerging talent had been evident both at the 2005 Confederations Cup in Germany and in the World Cup for which the Japanese were the first nation – after seeded hosts Germany – to secure a place in the finals. Japan won all six matches in the second round but struggled to maintain that momentum. It took an injury-time winner from Masashi Oguro to beat North Korea in their opening third-round game before they lost in Iran. Finally, they pulled themselves together and won their remaining four games to top the group.

"Now," warned Zico, "the hard work begins." As a veteran hero of three World Cups in the 1970s and 1980s, he should know.

STAR PLAYER
Hidetoshi Nakata
↗ Midfield ↗ Bolton Wanderers
↗ Born: January 22, 1977
Nakata is Japanese football's most successful export to Europe where he starred in Italy with Roma, Parma and Fiorentina before taking his hard-working game to the Premiership in 2005.

COACH
Zico (Artur Antunes Coimbra)
↗ Born: March 3, 1953 ↗ Appointed: July 2002
↗ Previous: Kashima Antlers

WORLD CUP RECORD

1930-50 did not enter	1966 did not enter
1954 did not qualify	1970-94 did not qualify
1958 did not enter	1998 1st round
1962 did not qualify	2002 2nd round

STAR PERFORMERS
Yoshikatsu Yamaguchi
↗ Goalkeeper ↗ Jubilo Iwata
↗ Born: August 15, 1975
Shunsuke Nakamura
↗ Midfield ↗ Celtic ↗ Born: June 24, 1978
Junichi Inamoto
↗ Midfield ↗ West Bromwich Albion
↗ Born: September 18, 1979
Shinji Ono
↗ Midfield ↗ Feyenoord
↗ Born: September 17, 1979
Takayuki Susuki
↗ Forward ↗ Kashima Antlers
↗ Born: June 5, 1976

THE ROAD TO THE FINALS

1st round	
Bye	
2nd round, group three	
W 1-0	home v Oman (Kubo)
W 2-1	away v Singapore (Takahara, Fujita)
W 7-0	home v India (Kubo, Fukunishi, Nakamura, Suzuki, Nakazawa 2, Ogasawara)
W 4-0	away v India (Suzuki, Ono, Fukunishi, Miyamoto)
W 1-0	away v Oman (Suzuki)
W 1-0	home v Singapore (Tamada)
3rd round, group B	
W 2-1	home v North Korea (Ogasawara, Oguro)
L 1-2	away v Iran (Fukunishi)
W 1-0	home v Bahrain (Salmeen og)
W 1-0	away v Bahrain (Ogasawara)
W 2-0	away v North Korea (Yanagisawa, Oguro)
W 2-1	home v Iran (Kaji, Oguro)

FRANCE

IN SEARCH OF LOST GLORY

Pride will drive France on – partly to make amends for their upset four years ago and partly to live up to the high standards Zinedine Zidane, Thierry Henry and their team-mates set for themselves in winning the World Cup eight years ago.

ABOVE: Footballing wizard Zinedine Zidane has come out of retirement to pull the strings in midfield.

WORLD CUP RECORD

1930 1st round	1974 did not qualify
1934 1st round	1978 1st round
1938 quarter-finals	1982 fourth place
1950 did not qualify	1986 third place
1954 1st round	1990 did not qualify
1958 third place	1994 did not qualify
1962 did not qualify	1998 champions
1966 1st round	2002 1st round
1970 did not qualify	

Briefly, the unthinkable was a realistic possibility. France left it until the very last moment. In the end, national coach Raymond Domenech breathed a massive sigh of relief after his star-studded team squeezed their way into the finals courtesy of a 4–0 demolition of Cyprus and Switzerland's simultaneous goalless draw with the Republic of Ireland.

But how far can the 1998 world champions go when the serious business begins in Germany? Much depends, as ever, on whether the French players can reproduce their club form on the international stage and recreate the spirit and style of the all-conquering unit who won the World Cup in 1998 and the European Championship two years later.

No one characterizes *Les Bleus* better than their captain Zinedine Zidane. The Real Madrid playmaker, who hung up his international boots after Euro 2004, came out of retirement to help France relaunch their qualifying hopes after they had run into serious trouble at the midway point of the Group Four campaign.

Zidane freely admits that the 1–1 draw with Switzerland in France's penultimate match was one of his worst-ever performances. But his status and genius is such that few doubt he can still guide his country on another high-flying World Cup adventure.

On paper the French still possess an awesome goalscoring unit. Thierry Henry is Arsenal's all-time record marksman, while David Trezeguet continues to prove with Juventus that he remains one of the most prolific marksmen in Europe. Liverpool's Djibril Cisse, despite spending much of his time battling for starting rights with both club and country, was top scorer in qualifying with four goals, while Sylvain Wiltord is enjoying a new lease of life since returning home to Lyon from Arsenal.

At the other end of the pitch, debate will continue all the way to Germany about whether Domenech should maintain faith in Lyon's Gregory Coupet as his goalkeeper or revert to the talismanic Fabien Barthez, one of the few surviving heroes of the world and European "double".

With Patrick Vieira still a massive influence in the heart of midfield, Domenech is certain his squad will be "mentally and collectively strong" enough to pose a serious threat to those other usual suspects vying for Brazil's title.

STAR PERFORMERS

William Gallas
↗ Central defender ↗ Chelsea
↗ Born: August 17, 1977

Claude Makelele
↗ Midfielder ↗ Chelsea
↗ Born: February 18, 1973

Patrick Vieira
↗ Midfielder ↗ Juventus
↗ Born: June 23, 1976

Zinedine Zidane
↗ Midfielder ↗ Real Madrid
↗ Born: June 23, 1972

David Trezeguet
↗ Striker ↗ Juventus
↗ Born: October 15, 1977

THE ROAD TO THE FINALS

D 0-0	home v Israel
W 2-0	away v Faroe Islands (Giuly, Cisse)
D 0-0	home v Rep Ireland
W 2-0	away v Cyprus (Wiltord, Henry)
D 0-0	home v Switzerland
D 1-1	away v Israel (Trezeguet)
W 3-0	home v Faroe Islands (Cisse 2, S Olsen og)
W 1-0	away v Rep Ireland (Henry)
D 1-1	away v Switzerland (Cisse)
W 4-0	home v Cyprus (Zidane, Wiltord, Dhorasoo, Giuly)

STAR PLAYER

Thierry Henry

↗ Striker ↗ Arsenal

↗ Born: August 17, 1977

Henry was originally a winger when his talent was nurtured by Arsene Wenger at Monaco. After a short unhappy spell at Juventus, he teamed up again with his original mentor at Arsenal and progressed from goal-scoring strength to strength. Henry, a young stalwart in the French 1998 World Cup and Euro 2000 double team, established himself earlier this season as Arsenal's all-time record marksman. Along the way he also became the Premiership's leading goalscorer twice in three seasons to make the £10.5m fee Arsenal paid in 1999 appear a bargain. In 2005 he became Arsenal's captain after the sale of compatriot Patrick Vieira to Juventus.

COACH

Raymond Domenech

↗ Born: January 24, 1952

It was second time lucky for Domenech when he was appointed national coach in 2004, having previously been overlooked in favour of Jacques Santini. The one-time midfielder from Lyon, Paris SG and Bordeaux had spent 11 enormously successful years as manager of the French Under-21s with whom he gained potentially crucial knowledge of the players now at his disposal.

Domenech, who succeeded Jacques Santini after the quarter-final exit at Euro 2004, says: "Brazil seem to be above every other team. They have this capacity to accelerate when they need to, they have so much power. But my boys have shown they can resist in difficult moments. They have never wavered. The goal is to go all the way. We want to be in Berlin on July 9."

That, of course, would rekindle memories of July 12, 1998, when *Les Bleus* ignited the whole of France as they took Brazil apart in the final and scored a sensational 3–0 victory on home soil. Millions of fans partied long into the night – and for several more days – to celebrate a performance marked by Zidane's brace of goals.

Sixty years earlier, France had hosted another World Cup. On that occasion they were less fortunate, going out in the quarter-finals to eventual champions Italy.

In the years that followed, France produced many great talents. In the 1980s, the likes of Michel Platini, Alain Giresse and Jean Tigana thrilled lovers of the beautiful game with their agility and flair. But France fell twice to Germany in consecutive World Cup semi-finals, first in a drama-laden thriller in Spain in 1982 and then in Mexico in 1986.

Founding members of FIFA, France have competed in 11 World Cup finals tournaments and the lethal Just Fontaine still holds the record of 13 goals in the finals, set in 1958.

All that was eclipsed by the glory of 1998 and the subsequent 2–1 defeat of Italy after Trezeguet's golden goal in the Euro 2000 final in Rotterdam.

Then, however, came the crash. At the 2002 World Cup in Korea and Japan, *Les Bleus* became the first holders to concede their crown without even scoring a goal. They lost to Senegal, drew with Uruguay and then succumbed to Denmark, before slinking off home in disgrace.

Coach Roger Lemerre was fired and replaced by Santini. Yet, despite a solid enough qualifying campaign for Euro 2004, the defending European champions failed to raise their game when it mattered.

Pride could prove a valuable weapon in Germany – and not only to make amends for events in Portugal two years ago. It was a Frenchman in Jules Rimet who established the World Cup and another Frenchman in Lucien Laurent who scored the first goal in the World Cup history book.

The challenge for Domenech is meeting the expectation that he and his players can write yet another page.

SWITZERLAND

BACK IN THE FRAME

Swiss put play-off bitterness behind them as Alexander Frei and Johan Vonlanthen lead the campaign to make up for a 12-year absence from the finals. At least veteran coach Kobi Kuhn knows his team will not be intimidated.

Switzerland may be one of central Europe's smaller countries and better known globally for cuckoo clocks, watches, skiing and chocolates but their footballers are not heading north just to make up the numbers.

The fact that the Swiss came through one of the toughest qualifying groups, joining France in the finals, after eliminating both the Republic of Ireland and Israel, then edging Turkey on away goals in a battle-scarred play-off, says a great deal about the quality of the current squad, many of whom play their club football in the Premier League, the Bundesliga and Serie A.

It also says a great deal about their mental strength, not least against the Turks – World Cup semi-finalists just four years ago – when the Swiss were intimidated on and off the field. In the end they needed goal difference to earn a place in the finals – their 2–0 first-leg lead almost cancelled out in Istanbul by a dramatic 4–2 Turkish victory.

The scenes at the end of the game as the Swiss players ran the gauntlet of Turkish fury both in leaving the pitch and in heading down the tunnel to the dressing rooms prompted a FIFA inquiry. But there was never any question at any point of the Swiss being barred from the finals as a result.

Marco Streller scored the decisive goal under enormous pressure in Istanbul as the Swiss earned a passage to Germany in defiance of Tuncay Sanli's hat-trick for the hosts.

Bayer Leverkusen midfielder Tranquillo Barnetta summed up the mood in the Swiss camp, saying: "We are a quality team and proved that we can deal with pressure. For me personally, World Cup qualification is the biggest thing on earth."

The Swiss are determined to play an active role on neighbouring German soil, not least as a dress rehearsal for the 2008 European Championships, which they are to host jointly with Austria.

For the country's veteran coach, Kobi Kuhn, qualification for Germany was thoroughly deserved. Kuhn says: "We feel we should be there. The Turkey

ABOVE: The Swiss team engulf Valon Behrami after he scores against Turkey in the Wankdorf.

STAR PERFORMERS

Pascal Zuberbuhler
↗ Goalkeeper ↗ Basel
↗ Born: January 8, 1971

Patrick Muller
↗ Central defender ↗ Basel
↗ Born: December 17, 1976

Johan Vogel
↗ Midfield ↗ PSV Eindhoven
↗ Born: March 8, 1977

Alexander Frei
↗ Forward ↗ Rennes
↗ Born: July 15, 1979

Johan Vonlanthen
↗ Forward ↗ Brescia
↗ Born: February 1, 1986

WORLD CUP RECORD

1930 did not qualify	1974 did not qualify
1934 quarter-finals	1978 did not qualify
1938 quarter-finals	1982 did not qualify
1950 1st round	1986 did not qualify
1954 quarter-finals	1990 did not qualify
1958 did not qualify	1994 1st round
1962 1st round	1998 did not qualify
1966 1st round	2002 did not qualify
1970 did not qualify	

THE ROAD TO THE FINALS

W 6-0	home v Faroe Islands (Vonlanthen 3, Frei 3)
D 1-1	home v Rep Ireland (Hakan Yakin)
D 2-2	away v Israel (Frei, Vonlanthen)
D 0-0	away v France
W 1-0	home v Cyprus (Frei)
W 3-1	away v Faroe Islands (Wicky, Frei 2)
D 1-1	home v Israel (Frei)
W 3-1	away v Cyprus (Frei, Senderos, Gygax)
D 1-1	home v France (Magnin)
D 0-0	away v Rep Ireland
Play-offs	
W 2-0	home v Turkey (Senderos, Behrami)
L 2-4	away v Turkey (Frei, Streller) Switzerland on away goals, 4-4 agg

COACH

Jakob 'Kobi' Kuhn

↗ Born: October 12, 1943

Kuhn was an outstanding midfield general in the 1960s with Switzerland and FC Zurich, scoring five goals in 62 internationals. He joined the federation's coaching staff in 1995 and finally rose to the position of national coach in July 2001. His appointment ended – successfully – an 11-year spell in which the Swiss had relied on foreign coaches without apparently realizing the answer to their problems was already in house.

STAR PLAYER

Hakan Yakin

↗ Midfield ↗ Young Boys Bern

↗ Born: February 22, 1977

Hakan is the younger of the two Yakin brothers, fellow international Murat being three years older. Hakan has been one of the finest Swiss players over the last decade and was a key member of the squad which used progress to the European Championship finals in Portugal in 2004 as a springboard to World Cup qualification. His skill and combative style have earned a host of admirers beyond Switzerland, but he has not always been fortunate in the way transfers to Galatasaray in Turkey, Paris Saint-Germain in France and Stuttgart in Germany have worked out. Bad luck with injuries has not helped. Going to Germany will give him the opportunity at least to prove his critics wrong.

match was a great experience for us – to come through after withstanding all that pressure. The lessons we learned and the maturity and togetherness we gained are going to stand us in good stead for the future."

That future will not, of course, include the likes of Ciri Sforza, Alain Sutter and the rest of the squad who took Switzerland to the 1994 tournament under the management of Englishman Roy Hodgson, since most have long since retired from international football.

Hamburg survivor Raphael Wicky believes the current squad are better equipped to hurt the opposition than the 1994 vintage which was the last Swiss squad to enjoy the excitement, drama and limelight of playing on the world game's biggest stage.

He says: "When we went to the finals in the United States, team spirit and collective play were the important factors, but we were a little limited. Now we have a lot of young players who express themselves on the pitch and who are already playing for big clubs abroad. We have more depth in the squad and more options should someone get injured."

That statement of faith represents significant progress since, at the finals of the European Championship in Portugal two years ago, Kuhn's side mustered one solitary goal and just the one point to exit at the group stage, finishing bottom of their group.

Nonetheless, Switzerland had their encouraging moments, with brothers Murat and Hakan Yakin providing the backbone and Johann Vogel and Wicky showing promise in midfield.

In Colombia-born centre-forward Johan Vonlanthen they also boast potentially one of the players of the tournament. The teenage striker from PSV Eindhoven has already entered the record books as the youngest-ever goalscorer in European Championship history and now – in partnership with France-based Alexander Frei – he is poised to make his mark at the very top level of the game.

In the inter-war years Switzerland were one of the major continental powers and ranked among the pre-tournament favourites for both the 1934 and the 1938 World Cups in which they reached the quarter-finals on each occasion. In those days they employed a defensive system known as the *Verrou* or "Swiss bolt".

No such revolutionary tactics are expected this time, though Kuhn does have a score to settle with the World Cup. When he went with Switzerland to play at the 1966 finals in England he was dropped from the team, along with two team-mates, for breaking curfew before their opening game against Germany.

Older and wiser, he is confident that none of his own players will let the side down – on or off the pitch.

SOUTH KOREA

ONWARDS AND UPWARDS

The Koreans' fourth-place finish in the last World Cup back home set a high standard for Dick Advocaat to match. But European-based heroes such as Park Ji Sung could prove even more dangerously effective than the team of four years ago.

STAR PLAYER
Ahn Jung Hwan
↗ Striker ↗ Metz
↗ Born: January 27, 1976
Attacking leader who wrote his name into Korean football history when he scored the golden goal which beat Italy in the 2002 second round – and was promptly sacked by his Serie A club, Perugia.

For a manager to be sacked for qualifying failure is nothing unusual. But to be sacked after successfully reaching the finals was the rare fate of Jo Bonfrere just seven days after South Korea wrapped up their campaign.

Bonfrere's "fault" lay in failing to generate the consistency of form the Koreans had shown under fellow Dutchman Guus Hiddink. In 2002 Hiddink had guided the World Cup co-hosts to the semi-finals and on to fourth place, the finest achievement by any Asian side.

When Hiddink returned to Europe with PSV Eindhoven he was succeeded first by Portuguese coach Humberto Coelho then by Bonfrere. Now guiding the Reds into their sixth successive finals is the task of yet another Dutchman.

On arriving in Seoul, former Holland boss Dick Advocaat made a bold statement. "We are going to try to go at least as far as in 2002. This is not mission impossible. The nucleus of the squad is still there but with four more years' experience – which has to be a plus."

This is Korea's seventh appearance in the finals and victories in the Asian cup (twice) and the Asian Games (three times) mark them out as the continent's greatest international achievers.

Not that they lived up to that reputation at the start of 2006 qualifying. Thus, after stuttering to a 2–0 home win over Lebanon then a goalless draw against minnows Maldives, the federation replaced Coelho with Bonfrere.

The reward for that brave change was a run of six wins in 10 games which sent the Koreans to Germany. Top scorer was the home-based striker Lee Dong Gook from Pohang Steelers. But equally significant contributions came from European-based players such as the left-back Lee Young Pyo and left winger Park Ji Sung, both of whom had initially followed Hiddink to PSV.

Goalkeeper Lee Woon Jae is heading towards a century of international appearances, while midfielder or winger Cha Du Ri is the son of Korea's first top-class export. Cha Bum Kun played in Germany in the 1980s with Eintracht Frankfurt – where his son was born and now plays. Whether this sort of home advantage will prove as inspiring as in 2002, of course, is another matter.

COACH
Dick Advocaat
↗ Born: September 27, 1947
↗ Appointed: September 2005
↗ Previous: Haarlem, SVV, Holland, PSV Eindhoven, Rangers, Borussia Monchengladbach, United Arab Emirates

WORLD CUP RECORD

1930-50 did not enter	1986 1st round
1954 1st round	1990 1st round
1958 did not enter	1994 1st round
1962 did not qualify	1998 1st round
1966 did not enter	2002 fourth place
1970-82 did not qualify	

STAR PERFORMERS

Lee Woon Jae
↗ Goalkeeper ↗ Suwon Samsung
↗ Born: April 26, 1973

Lee Young Pyo
↗ Left-back ↗ Tottenham Hotspur
↗ Born: April 23, 1977

Cha Du Ri
↗ Midfield ↗ Eintracht Frankfurt
↗ Born: July 25, 1980

Park Ji Sung
↗ Left wing ↗ Manchester United
↗ Born: February 25, 1981

Lee Dong Gook
↗ Forward ↗ Pohang Steelers
↗ Born: April 29, 1979

THE ROAD TO THE FINALS

1st round	
Bye	
2nd round, group seven	
W 2-0	home v Lebanon (Cha Du Ri, Cho Byung Kuk)
D 0-0	away v Maldives
W 2-0	home v Vietnam (Ahn Jung Hwan, Kim Do Heon)
W 2-1	away v Vietnam (Lee Dong Gook, Lee Chun Soo)
D 1-1	away v Lebanon (Choi Jin Cheul)
W 2-0	home v Maldives (Kim Do Heon, Lee Dong Gook)
3rd round, group A	
W 2-0	home v Kuwait (Lee Dong Gook, Lee Young Pyo)
L 0-2	away v Saudi Arabia
W 2-1	home v Uzbekistan (Lee Dong Pyo, Lee Dong Gook)
D 1-1	away v Uzbekistan (Park Chu Young)
W 4-0	away v Kuwait (Park Chu Young, Lee Dong Gook, Chung Kyung Ho, Park Ji Sung)
L 0-1	home v Saudi Arabia
W 2-1	home v Iran (Kaji, Oguro)

TOGO

WEST AFRICA'S HIGH FLYERS

Togo's Hawks dive onto the finals for the first time after taking their qualifying cue from top-scoring Arsenal striker Emmanuel Adebayor – and shocking African football by outwitting the 2002 heroes from Senegal.

Arsenal striker Emmanuel Sheyi Adebayor's 11 goals carried Togo to the finals for the first time and edged out 2002 quarter-finalists Senegal.

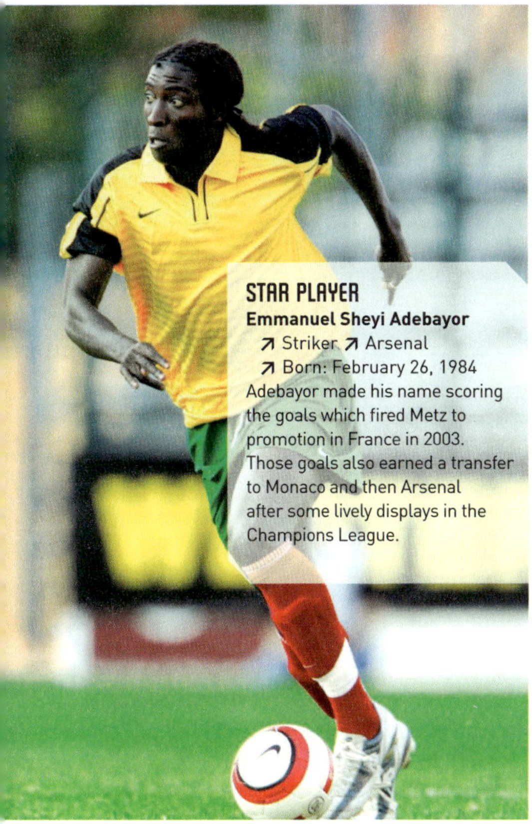

STAR PLAYER

Emmanuel Sheyi Adebayor

↗ Striker ↗ Arsenal

↗ Born: February 26, 1984

Adebayor made his name scoring the goals which fired Metz to promotion in France in 2003. Those goals also earned a transfer to Monaco and then Arsenal after some lively displays in the Champions League.

The Hawks clinched a ticket for Germany with a 3–2 win in Congo in their final game, to finish two points ahead of the Senegalese. Adebayor scored the first goal and Abdel Coubadja added two more after Congo had led twice.

But it was Togo's results against Senegal which held the key to topping the group. They won 3–1 at home then gained a crucial 2–2 draw in Dakar.

Adebayor is the country's most popular player with fan clubs all over the country. That is no surprise, given his prolific form in the qualifiers.

He netted twice in the 3–0 win over Liberia, hit the equaliser in Senegal, scored twice in a 4–1 win over Zambia, grabbed the winner against Mali, struck both goals in the 2–0 home win over Congo and scored the opener in the Hawks' vital home win over Senegal.

Another of Togo's Europe-based players is winger Junior Senaya who netted the other two goals in the win over Senegal. Senaya plays for Juventus – the Swiss second division club, rather than the Italian giants from Turin.

Togo suffered their only defeat in their opening game, 1–0 away to Zambia. In their next nine qualifiers, they won seven and drew two.

Their Nigerian coach, former World Cup defender Stephen Keshi, was rewarded with Togo's highest honour, the *Grand Commandeur dans l'Ordre du Merite*. He was the first foreigner to receive the award.

A power cut in the capital, Lome, put a temporary dampener on celebrations. But the Monday after the Hawks' qualification was declared a national holiday and 30,000 fans crammed into Kegue stadium for a public reception.

Togo's president, Rock Gnassingbe, said: "The Hawks are national heroes and I'm sure they can go on to cause even more surprises."

Following Togo's poor performances in the African Cup of Nations, coach Stephen Keshi was dismissed and replaced by the German Otto Pfister, who has had wide experience of managing in Africa with Zaire and Ghana U-17s, as well as club sides in Egypt and Tunisia. Pfister signed a short-term contract covering the World Cup finals.

WORLD CUP RECORD

1930-58 did not exist	1982 did not qualify
1962 not eligible	1986 did not qualify
1966 did not enter	1990 did not qualify
1970 did not enter	1994 did not qualify
1974 did not qualify	1998 did not qualify
1978 did not qualify	2002 did not qualify

COACH

Otto Pfister

↗ Born: 1939 ↗ Appointed: February 2006

↗ Previous: Zaire, Ghana U-17s, Saudi Arabia

STAR PERFORMERS

Kossi Agassa

↗ Goalkeeper ↗ Metz

↗ Born: July 2, 1978

Jean-Paul Abalo

↗ Defender ↗ Amiens

↗ Born: June 26, 1975

Adekamni Olufade

↗ Midfield ↗ Charleroi

↗ Born: January 7, 1980

Abdel Kader Coubadja

↗ Midfield/forward ↗ Sochaux

↗ Born: April 8, 1979

Junior Senaya

↗ Winger ↗ YF Juventus (Switzerland)

↗ Born: April 19, 1984

THE ROAD TO THE FINALS

1st round	
L 0-1	away v Equatorial Guinea
W 2-0	home v Equatorial Guinea (Adebayor, Salifou)
2nd round	
L 0-1	away v Zambia
W 3-1	home v Senegal (Adebayor, Senaya Junior 2)
D 0-0	away v Liberia
W 2-0	home v Congo (Adebayor 2)
W 1-0	home v Mali (Adebayor)
W 2-1	away v Mali (Salifou, Mamam)
W 4-1	home v Zambia (Adebayor 2, Mamam, Coubadja)
D 2-2	away v Senegal (Olufade, Adebayor)
W 3-0	home v Liberia (Adebayor 2, Mamam)
W 3-2	away v Congo (Adebayor, Coubadja 2)

SPAIN

MUST DO BETTER

The prize-winning class of Real Madrid and Barcelona must take a back seat as Raul, Iker Casillas and co try to prove once again that there is considerably more to Spanish football than their impressive achievements at club level.

Perennial underachievers and European football's biggest sleeping giants. That is Spain as they approach a major finals with little pedigree in terms of World Cup success and few experts daring to predict that they can even come anywhere near carrying off the trophy for the first time.

Yet this is a country which, at club level, rakes in title after title; a country which has produced some of the most naturally gifted players and most illustrious clubs in one of the finest leagues in the world. Yet, for some undefined reason, Spain fall short time and time again when it comes to mixing it at international level.

Frustratingly for their long-suffering fans, the national team never match the lofty heights scaled by the likes of Real Madrid and Barcelona. The prize-winning genius of foreign players from Di Stefano and Puskas, to Maradona and Cruyff and now Zidane and Ronaldinho has done nothing to inspire the national team.

Football historians must delve back more than 40 years to find their one and only international title: the 1964 European Championship.

Successive national coaches have failed to translate year after year of club success into international prizes. Fourth place at Brazil in 1950 remains Spain's best finish in the World Cup. Even when they hosted the tournament in 1982, they managed only one victory and scrambled only as far as the second phase.

Four years ago, as in countless other major competitions, Spain arrived in Korea and Japan as potential threats yet ended up leaving the Far East bitterly disappointed after losing to their Korean co-hosts in a quarter-final which also marked the end of an era for such stars as Luis Enrique and Fernando Hierro.

ABOVE: Spain's players celebrate their second goal in the play-off against Slovakia scored by Garcia.

Two years later, at Euro 2004 in neighbouring Portugal, when Spain arguably had their best chance of glory in decades and the backing of thousands of fans, they again failed to live up to expectations and suffered a

WORLD CUP RECORD

1930 did not enter	1974 did not qualify
1934 quarter-finals	1978 1st round
1938 did not enter	1982 2nd round
1950 fourth place	1986 quarter-finals
1954 did not qualify	1990 2nd round
1958 did not qualify	1994 quarter-finals
1962 1st round	1998 1st round
1966 1st round	2002 quarter-finals
1970 did not qualify	

STAR PERFORMERS

Carles Puyol
↗ Central defender ↗ Barcelona
↗ Born: April 13, 1978

Xavi (Full name Xavier Hernandez Creus)
↗ Midfield ↗ Barcelona
↗ Born: January 25, 1980

Juan Carlos Valeron
↗ Midfielder ↗ Deportivo de La Coruna
↗ Born: June 17, 1975

Raul (Full name Raul Gonzalez Blanco)
↗ Forward ↗ Real Madrid
↗ Born: June 27, 1977

Fernando Torres
↗ Striker ↗ Atletico Madrid
↗ Born March 20, 1984:

THE ROAD TO THE FINALS

D 1-1	away v Bosnia-Herzegovina (Vicente)
W 2-0	home v Belgium (Luque, Raul)
D 0-0	away v Lithuania
W 5-0	home v San Marino (Joaquin, Torres, Raul, Guti, Del Horno)
D 0-0	away v Serbia and Montenegro
W 1-0	home v Lithuania (Luque)
D 1-1	home v Bosnia-Herzegovina (Marchena)
D 1-1	home v Serbia and Montenegro (Raul)
W 2-0	away v Belgium (Torres 2)
W 6-0	away v San Marino (Lopez, Torres 3, Sergio Ramos 2)
Play-off	
W 5-1	home v Slovakia (Luis Garcia 3, Torres, Morientes)
D 1-1	away v Slovakia (Villa) Spain 6-2 on agg

STAR PLAYER

Iker Casillas

↗ Goalkeeper ↗ Real Madrid

↗ Born: May 20, 1981

Real Madrid may buy big from England, France, Argentina and Brazil but one of the fans' greatest favourites is local boy Casillas. He joined Madrid at eight and was a world youth champion with Spain 1999. A year later injury to German Bodo Illgner saw Casillas win his first Champions League in the all-Spanish final against Valencia. He played a key role, with some brilliant saves as substitute, in the 2002 Champions League final defeat of Bayer Leverkusen. That display earned him the role as Spain's No 1, after injury to Jose Canizares, at the subsequent World Cup finals – which he marked with an opening-match penalty stop from Slovenia's Milenko Acimovic.

COACH

Luis Aragones

↗ Born: July 28, 1938

Luis, as he was then known, was a Real Madrid cast-off who went on to score goals for neighbours Atletico Madrid and then coached them to victory in the World Club Cup in 1975. Also coached Valencia, Betis, Espanyol, Sevilla and Mallorca, before being appointed national boss in succession to Inaki Saez after the European Championship flop in Portugal in 2004.

further ignominious first-round exit.

Now the wily managerial veteran Luis Aragones faces the puzzle of bringing all the potential to fruition.

Judging by their qualifying campaign, it could be another hard slog. With the players at their disposal, Spanish teams should not have to qualify via the play-offs, as Aragones's men were forced to against Slovakia after finishing two points behind overall group winners Serbia and Montenegro. All too often during the qualifying campaign, despite winning or drawing every game, Spain's players failed to make their class tell.

Typical examples were the narrow 1–0 home win over Lithuania and the 1–1 home draw with Serbia and Montenegro when the advantage of skipper Raul Gonzalez's opening goal was squandered.

From Iker Casillas in goal to Raul leading the charge up front, the latest generation of Spaniards know only too well that once again they have the talent to banish once and for all the stain of past failures. Whether they will is another matter entirely.

Raul's contribution is open to question. The Real Madrid sharpshooter suffered a serious knee injury when he miscued a shot during his side's 3–0 defeat by arch-rivals Barcelona in November and is battling to regain fitness in time.

Should he fail to recover, it will leave a greater burden than ever on his old friend, the Liverpool striker Fernando Morientes, and another Anfield exile in winger Luis Garcia who struck a dramatic hat-trick in the play-off demolition of Slovakia.

With the likes of Xabi Alonso, Xavi and Juan Carlos Valeron in midfield plus Joaquin on the right wing, Spain could cut loose in Germany.

Knowing the qualities of his squad means Aragones, who led Spain into the finals on the back of an 18-match unbeaten streak, can afford to be positive.

He says: "Spain have qualified for every World Cup in the last 30 years. That means that for us qualification is something we can consider to be normal. But we want to get closer to the winners and get closer to the stronger teams. Perhaps we're not as physically strong as other sides but we make up for it with our technical qualities.

"Brazil are head and shoulders above the rest. But Brazil aside, I think Spain are closer to the next group – teams like Argentina, England and Germany. All we need to do is learn to compete with them. Why haven't we done it yet? I can't say but we do have a lot of technically gifted young players coming through . . ."

Perhaps, at long last, it is time for those gifts to pay off.

UKRAINE

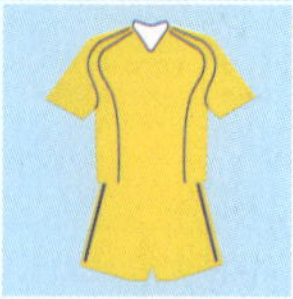

THE YELLOW REVOLUTION

Ukraine are in the finals for the first time at only the third attempt. Their dreams now rest not on beginner's luck, but on one of the world's most lethal marksmen and a manager who has been to the finals as a player himself.

Ukraine, having slipped up twice previously in the play-offs, finally held their nerve to become the first European nation – after the hosts, of course – to secure their place in the finals in Germany.

Qualifying was a personal triumph for high-profile striker and top scorer in the group campaign, Andriy Shevchenko. He had an extra reason for celebrating after Ukraine were sure: Shevchenko had promised himself a first finals appearance to make amends for fluffing the crucial penalty that condemned Milan to their sensational Champions League defeat by Liverpool only months earlier.

Now, Ukraine can dream of emulating Croatia, another of the new eastern European nations who, released from Iron Curtain shackles, finished third on their World Cup debut in 1998.

Ukraine was one of the 15 republics comprising the Soviet Union until freedom in December 1991 followed the communist collapse. The football federation secured autonomy of its own just too late to enter the 1994 World Cup, and thus Ukraine made their debut in the 1998 preliminaries.

They finished second behind Germany, but lost 3–1 on aggregate to the glory-bound Croats in the play-offs.

Again, in the 2002 qualifiers, Ukraine finished runners-up in their group behind neighbouring Poland, but were unlucky enough to be drawn in the play-offs against the Germans – the strongest possible opponents – and went down 4–1.

Subsequent failure in the Euro 2004 qualifiers led to the predictable fall-out, with Leonid Buryak being replaced as national coach by his former Soviet and Dynamo Kiev team-mate Oleh Blokhin.

The backbone of Blokhin's squad contains far-reaching experience, notably in midfield through the contrasting talents of Anatoliy Tymoshchuk and Andriy Husin, with around 100 caps between them. At the back, goalkeeper Olexandr Shovkovskyi, after an erratic start to his international career, provides the security.

Attack, of course, is where Ukraine shine – and not only through

WORLD CUP RECORD

1930-1990 did not exist
1994 did not enter
1998 did not qualify
2002 did not qualify

STAR PERFORMERS

Olexander Shovkovskiy
↗ Goalkeeper ↗ Dynamo Kiev
↗ Born: January 2, 1975

Andriy Nesmachniy
↗ Defender ↗ Dynamo Kiev
↗ Born: February 28, 1979

Anatoliy Tymoshchuk
↗ Midfielder ↗ Shakhtar Donetsk
↗ Born: March 30, 1979

Andriy Husin
↗ Midfielder ↗ K S Samara
↗ Born: December 11, 1972

Andriy Voronin
↗ Forward ↗ Bayer Leverkusen
↗ Born: July 21, 1979

THE ROAD TO THE FINALS

D 1-1	away v Denmark (Husin)
W 2-1	away v Kazakhstan (Bielik, Rotan)
D 1-1	home v Greece (Shevchenko)
W 2-0	home v Georgia (Bielik, Shevchenko)
W 3-0	away v Turkey (Husev, Shevchenko 2)
W 2-0	away v Albania (Rusol, Husin)
W 1-0	home v Demmark (Voronin)
W 2-0	home v Kazakhstan (Shevchenko, Avdeyev og)
W 1-0	away v Greece (Husin)
D 1-1	away v Georgia (Rotan)
L 0-1	home v Turkey
D 2-2	home v Albania [Shevchenko, Rotan]

BELOW: Andriy Husin scores against European champions Greece in Piraeus and Ukraine are on their way to the finals in Germany.

COACH

Oleh Blokhin

↗ Born: November 5, 1952

Blokhin was a star outside-left for the former Soviet Union while the Ukraine – and his long-term club, Dynamo Kiev – were within the USSR. He scored 211 goals in 431 games and 47 goals in a record 112 internationals. He was also voted European Footballer of the Year in 1975. Blokhin's fame provided him with a launch pad into club coaching in Greece before he returned to Ukraine in 2003 to succeed Leonid Buryak as national coach.

STAR PLAYER

Andriy Shevchenko

↗ Striker ↗ AC Milan

↗ Born: September 29, 1976

Shevchenko made his international mark when he converted the decisive penalty in Milan's shoot-out victory over Juventus in the 2003 Champions League Final. Until then, he had missed out on the big occasions through Ukraine's repeated failures in World Cup and Euro qualifying. Not that Shevchenko was at fault. His marksmanship meant he was five times Ukraine champion with Kiev before joining Milan in 1999. He was then 24-goal top scorer in Serie A in 2000 and 2004 when he was also voted European Footballer of the Year. The sole black mark was a crucial penalty failure in Milan's shoot-out defeat by Liverpool in the 2005 Champions League final.

Shevchenko. Initially, he flourished for both club and country in partnership with Serhiy Rebrov, but then struggled for support after the latter's ill-starred departure for English football and Tottenham Hotspur.

Now Blokhin has redesigned Ukraine's tactics so that Shevchenko no longer leans on one partner but benefits from the varying pace and interpassing angles offered by the Shakhtar Donetsk striker Andriy Vorobey and Bayer Leverkusen's back-in-favour Andriy Voronin.

Ukraine were comparatively slow starters in the group. They drew two of their opening three matches and, in between, only just scraped a 2–1 home win over Kazakhstan who were making their competitive debut as a European nation after transferring from the Asian confederation.

Shevchenko opened his scoring account in the third match, a 1–1 home draw against newly crowned European champions Greece.

After that, however, he was hard to stop. He struck three times in two matches against Georgia and Turkey as Ukraine embarked on a six-match winning streak which fired them to the top of the table.

With their pursuers hard at work taking points off each other, Shevchenko and co were left needing to win away to Georgia in their penultimate match to make history.

The occasion in the national stadium in Tbilisi was an eerie one because all fans were barred on FIFA orders after hooligan violence at previous Georgian home games against Greeks and Turks. Ukraine, so close to their goal, were nervy and jittery in both defence and attack. Ruslan Rotan put them ahead just before half-time but wasted a second-half chance to make the game safe. He held his head in his hands as Georgi Gakhokidze snatched a late equaliser.

At the final whistle the Ukrainians thought they had failed and would still need a point at home to Turkey.

Two hours later, however, their depression turned to screaming, shouting delight. Danish substitute Soren Larsen became the hero of Ukraine by scoring a stoppage-time equaliser which saw Denmark hold Turkey 2–2. Ukraine were confirmed as group-winners with a couple of games in hand.

"That was such a big game for us," said Blokhin during a brief pause in the partying. "But it was so difficult without the crowd atmosphere. It's not like a proper football match without fans in the stadium. I think in a 'proper' atmosphere we would have played better and won the game to qualify without needing to wait for the Danes.

"A lot of people called me unrealistic when I said after the original draw that I was confident we would reach the finals. I know they will call me much worse – even crazy – but I also now believe we can win the World Cup itself."

Blokhin is the one member of the party who has been there before, having reached the second round in 1982 and 1986. But that was with the Soviet Union. National pride was never quite like this.

TUNISIA

MEN WITH A MISSION

Tunisia are trying to get past the first round for the first time ever, but boss Roger Lemerre believes his team boast the experience, pride and all-round talent to make a fourth consecutive appearance in the finals their best yet.

STAR PLAYER

Francileudo Santos

↗ Striker ↗ Toulouse

↗ Born: March 20, 1979

Santos, who was born in Brazil but made his name as a footballer in France, was a key figure in Tunisia's 2004 African Nations' triumph, and followed this up by top-scoring with six goals in their World Cup qualifying campaign.

Few of the worldwide qualifying programmes produced a climax quite like the one that saw Roger Lemerre's Tunisia dramatically snatch an eleventh-hour place in the finals for the fourth successive time.

In their very last game in front of 60,000 passionate fans, Tunisia took on their most ardent North African rivals Morocco knowing that a draw would fulfil their dreams, but defeat would hand a finals ticket to their neighbours.

Twice Lemerre's team came from behind to rescue a 2–2 draw in that final, nail-biting encounter and the French coach, already revered for having led Tunisia to their first African Nations Cup triumph in 2004, has now taken on hero status.

It's all a far cry from the dark days when he was sacked as national coach of his native France after their great triumph at Euro 2000 was followed by disaster in the first round of the 2002 World Cup finals.

Now Lemerre is back on the big stage, he can bring all his considerable experience to bear on preparing to perfection the Carthage Eagles, the first African country ever to win a match in the finals when they downed Mexico in 1978.

WORLD CUP RECORD

1930-54 did not exist	1982 did not qualify
1958 not eligible	1986 did not qualify
1962 did not qualify	1990 did not qualify
1966 did not enter	1994 1st round
1970 did not qualify	1998 1st round
1974 did not qualify	2002 1st round
1978 1st round	

STAR PERFORMERS

Hatem Trabelsi

↗ Defender ↗ Ajax Amsterdam

↗ Born: January 25, 1977

Jose Clayton

↗ Defender ↗ Esperance

↗ Born: March 21, 1974

Kaies Ghodbare

↗ Midfielder ↗ Samsunspor

↗ Born: January 7, 1976

Adel Chedli

↗ Midfielder ↗ Istres

↗ Born: September 16, 1976

Haykel Guemamdia

↗ Forward ↗ Strasbourg

↗ Born: December 22, 1981

COACH

Roger Lemerre

↗ Born: June 18, 1941 ↗ Appointed: October 2002

↗ Previous: Lens, Racing Paris, Strasbourg, Esperance Tunis, France

On paper they are the most experienced of the five African nations in Germany, yet they still await their second victory in the competition. In 1998, they lost to England and Colombia and drew with Romania. Four years ago, they again picked up one solitary point.

Their 2004 African Nations success, combined with Lemerre's knowhow, should stand them in good stead. He says: "Our start to the campaign was not excellent. We had only five points from three games and we were even bottom of our group. Then we lost in Guinea when all of us were below par. But we refused to give up and then our record was almost perfect."

Experience runs through the side from Hatem Trabelsi and Jose Clayton at the back to Kaeis Ghodbane – who also comes up with valuable goals – in midfield and national hero Francileudo Santos in attack.

Lemerre says: "We have some good players. None of them are among the best in the world but their attitude sets them apart from other teams. They can be great ambassadors for Tunisian football in particular and for African football in particular. I feel we are on a mission."

THE ROAD TO THE FINALS

1st round – bye

2nd round

W 4-1	home v Botswana (Ribabro, Hagui 2, Zitouni)
L 1-2	away v Guinea (Braham)
D 1-1	away v Morocco (Santos)
D 2-2	away v Malawi (Jaziri, Ghodbane)
W 7-0	home v Malawi (Guemamdia, Santos 4, Clayton, Ghodbane)
W 3-1	away v Botswana (Nafti, Santos, Abdi)
W 2-0	home v Guinea (Clayton, Chadli)
W 1-0	home v Tunisia (Guemamdia)
W 2-0	away v Kenya (Guemamdia, Jomaa)
D 2-2	home v Morocco (Clayton, Chadli)

SAUDI ARABIA

THE BLIP FACTOR

The Saudis have a date with destiny to prove that their poor showing last time was just a blip in football history. Star striker Sami Al Jaber may be the man to fire up a new World Cup adventure for boss Marcos Paqueta.

Saeed Al Owairan put Saudi Arabia on the World Cup map when he scored one of the finals' greatest solo goals against Belgium in 1994, during the first of what will now be four consecutive appearances.

Unfortunately, the Saudis – despite their qualifying successes – have not pushed on from there. For all their initial investment in facilities and one of the finest stadia in the Middle East, the football-mad Saudis have struggled to keep necessary pace with the game's globalisation.

A reluctance to import foreign players and even greater reluctance to allow their own stars to play abroad has put them at a disadvantage when it comes to appearing on the mainstream international stage.

The Saudis won the World Youth Cup in Scotland in 1989 and their players possess the technical ability to compete with the best.

Experience on the global stage was demonstrably missing, however, in their first-round failures in 1998 and 2002 when they lost all but one of their six games. The worst beating was the 8–0 thrashing by Germany in their opening match in 2002, which prompted the inevitable departure of coach Nasser Al Johar.

Running the team now is Brazilian Marcos Paqueta, a former world youth title-winning coach. He became the 15th coach signed up by the Saudi federation in 10 years when he surprisingly replaced the Argentine Gabriel Calderon last December, 10 days after the draw for the finals.

Calderon had appeared to have worked well in instilling both morale and tactical discipline.

The Saudis conceded just one goal while winning all six games in their opening qualifying round, and again conceded only once in the second round when they won four games and drew the other two.

Defending that unbeaten record at the finals will be the responsibility of a team headed by a player, in Sami Al Jaber, worthy to have succeeded to the leadership mantle once worn by the great Majid Muhammed, the so-called "Pele of the Desert".

Al Jaber scored a hat-trick against Iran when the Saudis made their finals debut in 1994 and is now poised to join the handful of international superstars, such as Pele, who have appeared in four finals tournaments.

STAR PLAYER

Sami Al Jaber

↗ Forward ↗ Al Hilal

↗ Born: December 11, 1972

Jaber is a one-time captain of the Saudis who also became their first export when he played briefly in England with Wolves. Led the Saudi attacks in their appearances at the finals of 1994, 1998 and 2002.

COACH

Marcos Paqueta (Marcos Cesar Dias de Castro)

↗ Born: August 27, 1958

↗ Appointed: December 2005

↗ Previous: Brazil Under-17s and Under-20s, Avai, Al-Hilal (Saudi Arabia)

THE ROAD TO THE FINALS

1st round	
Bye	
2nd round, group eight	
W 3-0	home v Indonesia (Ibrahim Al Shahrani 2, Al Qahtani)
W 1-0	away v Sri Lanka (Ibrahim Al Shahrani)
W 3-0	home v Turkmenistan (Al Meshal 2, Noor Hawsawi)
W 1-0	away v Turkmenistan (Al Qahtani)
W 3-1	away v Indonesia (Al Meshal, Sulaimani, Al Qahtani)
W 3-0	home v Sri Lanka (Al Shlhoub 2, Fallata)
3rd round, group B	
D 1-1	away v Uzbekistan (Al Jaber)
W 2-0	home v South Korea (Khariri, Al Qahtani)
D 0-0	away v Kuwait
W 3-0	home v Kuwait (Al Shlhoub 2, S Al Harthi)
W 3-0	home v Uzbekistan (Al Jaber 2, Al Meshal)
W 1-0	away v South Korea (Al Anbar)

STAR PERFORMERS

Mohammed Al Deayea

↗ Goalkeeper ↗ Al Hilal

↗ Born: August 2, 1972

Ridha Tukar

↗ Defender ↗ Al Ittihad

↗ Born: November 29, 1975

Mohammed Al Shloub

↗ Midfield ↗ Al Hilal

↗ Born: December 9, 1980

Ibrahim Al Shahrani

↗ Midfield ↗ Al Ahli ↗ Born: July 21, 1974

Yasser Al Qahtani

↗ Forward ↗ Al Qadissiya

↗ Born: October 19, 1982

WORLD CUP RECORD

1930-74 did not enter	1998 1st round
1978-90 did not qualify	2002 1st round
1994 2nd round	

WORLD CUP STATS

WORLD CUP ATTENDANCES 1930-2002

Year	Host nation	Teams	Matches	Total atts	Ave att
1930	Uruguay	13	18	434,000	24,111
1934	Italy	16	17	395,000	23,235
1938	France	15	18	483,000	26,833
1950	Brazil	13	22	1,337,000	60,773
1954	Switzerland	16	26	943,000	36,269
1958	Sweden	16	35	868,000	24,800
1962	Chile	16	32	776,000	24,250
1966	England	16	32	1,614,677	50,459
1970	Mexico	16	32	1,673,975	52,312
1974	West Germany	16	38	1,774,022	46,685
1978	Argentina	16	38	1,610,215	42,374
1982	Spain	24	52	1,856,277	35,698
1986	Mexico	24	52	2,407,431	46,297
1990	Italy	24	52	2,517,348	48,411
1994	United States	24	52	3,587,538	68,991
1998	France	32	64	2,785,100	43,517
2002	South Korea/Japan	32	64	2,722,390	42,537

THE FIRST

Goal

Lucien Laurent (France) v Mexico, 1930

Own goal

Manuel Rosas (Mexico) v Chile, 1930

Hat-trick

Guillermo Stabile (Argentina) v Mexico, 1930

Expulsion

Placido Galindo (Peru) v Romania, 1930

Goalkeeper sent off

Gianluca Pagliuca (Italy) v Norway, 1994

Shoot-out

West Germany v France, 3-3, 5-4 pens (1982 semi-final)

THE FASTEST

Expulsion

Jose Batista (Uruguay) 56 seconds v Scotland, 1986

Goal

Hakan Sukur (Turkey) 11 seconds v S Korea, 2002

MOST WINS

Brazil	5
Germany /West Germany	3
Italy	3
Argentina	2
Uruguay	2
France	1
England	1

MOST TOURNAMENTS (TEAM)

Brazil 17

MOST TOURNAMENTS (PLAYER)

Antonio Carbajal (Mexico)
Lothar Matthaus (W Germany) **5 each**

RECORD MATCH ATTENDANCE

199,854 (Brazil v Uruguay, 1950)

YOUNGEST AND OLDEST

Youngest World Cup winner

Pele (Brazil) 17 years 249 days (v Sweden, 1958)

Youngest player

Norman Whiteside (N Ireland) 17 years 42 days (v Yugoslavia, 1982)

Youngest scorer

Pele (Brazil) 17 years 239 days (v Wales, 1958)

Oldest World Cup winner

Dino Zoff (Italy) 40 years 133 days (v W Germany, 1982)

Oldest player

Roger Milla (Cameroon) 42 years 39 days (v Russia, 1994)

Oldest scorer

Roger Milla (Cameroon) 42 years 39 days (v Russia, 1994)

THE HIGHEST

Goal aggregate per game

12	Austria v Switzerland 7-5 (1954)
11	Brazil v Poland 6-5 (1938)
11	Hungary v West Germany 8-3 (1954)

Goals per team per match

10	Hungary v El Salvador 10-1 (1982)
9	Hungary v S Korea 9-0 (1954)
9	Yugoslavia v Zaire 9-0 (1974)

Goals per team per tournament

27	Hungary (1954)
25	West Germany (1954)
23	France (1958)

Goals per tournament

13	Just Fontaine (France, 1958)
11	Sandor Kocsis (Hungary, 1954)
9	Ademir (Brazil, 1950), Eusebio (Portugal, 1966), Gerd Muller (West Germany, 1970)

Individual goals aggregate

14	Gerd Muller (West Germany)
13	Just Fontaine (France)
12	Pele (Brazil)
12	Ronaldo (Brazil)
11	Sandor Kocsis (Hungary)
11	Jurgen Klinsmann (West Germany)
10	Gabriel Batistuta (Argentina)
10	Gary Lineker (England)
10	Teofile Cubillas (Peru)
10	Grzegorz Lato (Poland)
10	Helmut Rahn (West Germany)

Individual goals per game

5	Oleg Salenko (Russia)
4	Ademir (Brazil)
4	Sandor Kocsis (Hungary)
4	Just Fontaine (France)
4	Ernst Wilimowski (Poland)
4	Eusebio (Portugal)
4	Emilio Butragueno (Spain)
4	Juan Alberto Schiaffino (Uruguay)

GOAL SCORING

Goals per game

Year	Host nation	Matches	Goals	Ave
1930	Uruguay	18	70	3.89
1934	Italy	17	70	4.12
1938	France	18	84	4.67
1950	Brazil	22	88	4.00
1954	Switzerland	26	140	5.38
1958	Sweden	35	126	3.60
1962	Chile	32	89	2.78
1966	England	32	89	2.78
1970	Mexico	32	95	2.97
1974	West Germany	38	97	2.55
1978	Argentina	38	102	2.68
1982	Spain	52	146	2.81
1986	Mexico	52	132	2.54
1990	Italy	52	115	2.21
1994	United States	52	141	2.71
1998	France	64	171	2.67
2002	Korea, Japan	64	161	2.52

TOP SCORER(S) PER TOURNAMENT

Year	Host	Top scorer	Goals
1930	Uruguay	Guillermo Stabile (Argentina)	8
1934	Italy	Oldrich Nejedly (Czechoslovakia)	4
1938	France	Leonidas (Brazil)	8
1950	Brazil	Ademir (Brazil)	8
1954	Switzerland	Sandor Kocsis (Hungary)	11
1958	Sweden	Just Fontaine (France)	13
1962	Chile	Garrincha (Brazil), Vava (Brazil), Leonel Sanchez (Chile), Drazan Jerkovic (Yugoslavia), Florian Albert (Hungary), Valentin Ivanov (Soviet Union)	4
1966	England	Eusebio (Portugal)	9
1970	Mexico	Gerd Muller (West Germany)	9
1974	West Germany	Grzegorz Lato (Poland)	7
1978	Argentina	Mario Kempes (Argentina)	6
1982	Spain	Paolo Rossi (Italy)	6
1986	Mexico	Gary Lineker (England)	6
1990	Italy	Salvatore Schillaci (Italy)	6
1994	United States	Oleg Salenko (Russia), Hristo Stoichkov (Bulgaria)	6
1998	France	Davor Suker (Croatia)	6
2002	South Korea/Japan	Ronaldo (Brazil)	8

LANDMARK GOALS

No	Player	Against	Year
1	Lucien Laurent (France)	Mexico	1930
100	Angelo Schiavio (Italy)	United States	1934
200	Tore Keller (Sweden)	Cuba	1938
300	Chico (Brazil)	Spain	1950
400	Max Morlock (West Germany)	Turkey	1954
500	Bobby Collins (Scotland)	Paraguay	1958
600	Drazan Jerkovic (Yugoslavia)	Uruguay	1962
700	Pak Seung Zing (North Korea)	Chile	1966
800	Gerd Muller (West Germany)	Bulgaria	1970
900	Hector Yazalde (Argentina)	Haiti	1974
1000	Rob Rensenbrink (Holland)	Scotland	1978
1100	Sergei Baltacha (Soviet Union)	New Zealand	1982
1200	Jean-Pierre Papin (France)	Canada	1986
1300	Gary Lineker (England)	Paraguay	1986
1400	Johnny Ekstrom (Sweden)	Costa Rica	1990
1500	Claudio Caniggia (Argentina)	Nigeria	1994
1600	Pierre Issa (own goal for France)	South Africa	1998
1700	Oliver Bierhoff (Germany)	Iran	1998
1800	Beto (Portugal)	United States	2002
1900	Christian Vieri (Italy)	South Korea	2002

SHOOT-OUT RECORD PER TEAM

Year	Host	Round	Match	Score
1982	Spain	Semi	West Germany v France	3-3, 5-4pens
1986	Mexico	Quarter	France v Brazil	1-1, 4-3pens
		Quarter	West Germany v Mexico	0-0, 4-1pens
		Quarter	Belgium v Spain	1-1, 5-4pens
1990	Italy	2nd	Rep Ireland v Romania	0-0, 5-4pens
		2nd	Argentina v Yugoslavia	0-0, 3-2pens
		Semi	Argentina v Italy	1-1, 4-3pens
		Semi	West Germany v England	1-1, 4-3pens
1994	USA	2nd	Bulgaria v Mexico	1-1, 3-1pens
		Quarter	Sweden v Romania	1-1, 5-4pens
		Final	Brazil v Italy	0-0, 3-2pens
1998	France	2nd	Argentina v England	2-2, 4-3pens
		Quarter	France v Italy	0-0, 4-3pens
		Semi	Brazil v Holland	1-1, 4-2pens
2002	S Korea	2nd	Spain v Rep Ireland	1-1, 3-2pens
2002	S Korea	Quarter	South Korea v Spain	0-0, 5-3pens

DISCIPLINE

Expulsions per tournament

Year	Host	No
1930	Uruguay	1
1934	Italy	1
1938	France	4
1950	Brazil	0
1954	Switzerland	3
1958	Sweden	3
1962	Chile	6
1966	England	5
1970	Mexico	0
1974	West Germany	5
1978	Argentina	3
1982	Spain	5
1986	Mexico	8
1990	Italy	16
1994	United States	15
1998	France	22
2002	South Korea/Japan	17

Expulsions per team

Argentina	9
Brazil	9
Cameroon	7
Germany/West Germany	6
Uruguay	6
Hungary	5
Italy	5
Mexico	5
Czechoslovakia	4
France	4
Holland	4
Bulgaria	3
Denmark	3
Soviet Union	3
Belgium	2
Bolivia	2
Chile	2
England	2
Paraguay	2
Portugal	2
South Korea	2
Sweden	2
Turkey	2
United States	2
Yugoslavia	2

1 each: Australia, Austria, Canada, China, Croatia, Honduras, Iraq, Jamaica, Northern Ireland, Peru, Romania, Saudi Arabia, Scotland, Senegal, Slovenia, South Africa, Spain, United Arab Emirates, Zaire.

PENALTY SHOOTOUTS

Shoot-out record per team

Team	Won-lost
West Germany	3-0
Argentina	3-0
Brazil	2-1
France	2-1
South Korea	1-0
Bulgaria	1-0
Belgium	1-0
Sweden	1-0
Rep Ireland	1-1
Spain	1-2
Holland	0-1
Yugoslavia	0-1
England	0-2
Mexico	0-2
Romania	0-2
Italy	0-3

WORLD CUP HISTORY

FOOTBALL'S BIGGEST STAGE

The World Cup finals give fans an insight into the state of global football like nothing else. What new laws have FIFA introduced? Which new stars are making the breakthrough? What tactics are in favour? The rest of football will be paying attention to all the innovations.

World football's organizing body, FIFA, was formed in 1904 and Jules Rimet became its president in 1921.

In 1928, at a special conference in Amsterdam, Jules Rimet and Henri Delaunay, General Secretary of the French Football Federation, proposed that FIFA hold a tournament every four years open to any country. The World Cup was born.

Thirteen nations took part in the first World Cup in Uruguay in 1930, with only four countries making the long ocean crossing from Europe.

This World Cup had an element of the Keystone Kops about it. Running on to treat a player in the semi-final against Argentina, the US trainer tripped and fell, breaking a bottle of chloroform. He was carried off unconscious. With France fighting back at 1–0 against Argentina, the referee blew the final whistle six minutes early. A near riot forced play to start again but Argentina held on to win. Football's greatest competition was up and running...

1930 URUGUAY

FIFA's French president Jules Rimet saw his dream come to life when Uruguay both hosted and won the inaugural World Cup. Only four European nations dared the long sea crossing. Continental powers such as Italy, Austria, Hungary and Czechoslovakia stayed away and the British home nations had already quit FIFA in a row over amateurism. Uruguay had won hosting rights by promising to build a new stadium and pay all travel costs as part of their centenary celebrations. France opened the tournament with a 4–1 win over Mexico despite losing goalkeeper Alex Thepot through injury after only 10 minutes. Inside forward Lucien Laurent scored the historic first goal. However, the group was ultimately won by Argentina who then thrashed the United States 6–1 in the semi-finals. Hosts Uruguay, also the reigning Olympic champions, defeated Yugoslavia by the same score in the other semi. Tension ran so high ahead of the final that fans were searched for firearms before the Uruguayans hit back from 2–1 down to win the first final 4–2.

POOL 1

France	4	Mexico	1
Argentina	1	France	0
Chile	3	Mexico	0
Chile	1	France	0
Argentina	6	Mexico	3
Argentina	3	Chile	1

	P	W	D	L	F	A	Pts
Argentina	3	3	0	0	10	4	6
Chile	3	2	0	1	5	3	4
France	3	1	0	2	4	3	2
Mexico	3	0	0	3	4	13	0

POOL 2

Yugoslavia	2	Brazil	1
Yugoslavia	4	Bolivia	0
Brazil	4	Bolivia	0

	P	W	D	L	F	A	Pts
Yugoslavia	2	2	0	0	6	1	4
Brazil	2	1	0	1	5	2	2
Bolivia	2	0	0	2	0	8	0

POOL 3

Romania	3	Peru	1
Uruguay	1	Peru	0
Uruguay	4	Romania	0

	P	W	D	L	F	A	Pts
Uruguay	2	2	0	0	5	0	4
Romania	2	1	0	1	3	5	2
Peru	2	0	0	2	1	4	0

POOL 4

USA	3	Belgium	0
USA	3	Paraguay	0
Paraguay	1	Belgium	0

	P	W	D	L	F	A	Pts
USA	2	2	0	0	6	0	4
Paraguay	2	1	0	1	1	3	2
Belgium	2	0	0	2	0	4	0

SEMI FINALS

Argentina	6	USA	1
Uruguay	6	Yugoslavia	1

FINAL – JULY 30: CENTENARIO, MONTEVIDEO

Uruguay 4 (Dorado 12, Cea 57, Iriarte 68, Castro 90) **Argentina 2** (Peucelle 20, Stabile 37)
HT: 1–2. Att: 93,000. Ref: Langenus (Belgium)
Uruguay: Ballestreros - Nasazzi, Mascheroni - Andrade, Fernandez, Gestido - Dorado, Scarone, Castro, Cea, Iriarte.
Argentina: Botasso - Della Torre, Paternoster - Evaristo, Monti, Suarez - Peucelle, Varallo, Stabile, Ferreira, Evaristo.
Top scorer: 8 Stabile (Argentina)

1934 ITALY

Italy emulated Uruguay by winning the second World Cup as hosts. Angry that Europe had snubbed their party in 1930, the Uruguayans, stayed away. Dictator Benito Mussolini had demanded that his organising officials and players use the event to demonstrate the superiority of Italy's fascist system. That he got his way was due partly to the shrewd management of Vittorio Pozzo and partly to the intimidatory effect of the atmosphere on several referees – notably in the quarter-final victory over Spain. Austria's famed Wunderteam, led by the great Matthias Sindelar, proved too old and fragile for the challenge and lost to the Italians in the semi-finals. Czechoslovakia came through the other side of the draw, inspired by their left-wing partnership of Oldrich Nejedly and Antonin Puc. In the final Puc gave the Czechs the lead only for Italy to equalise nine minutes from time through Raimundo Orsi, who had been a final loser with Argentina four years earlier. Italy's flagging veteran centre-forward Angelo Schiavio won it for the hosts in extra time.

FIRST ROUND

* After extra time ® Replay

Italy	7	USA	1
Czechoslovakia	2	Romania	1
Germany	5	Belgium	2
Austria	3	France	2*
Spain	3	Brazil	1
Switzerland	3	Holland	2
Sweden	3	Argentina	2
Hungary	4	Egypt	2

SECOND ROUND

Germany	2	Sweden	1
Austria	2	Hungary	1
Italy	1	Spain	1*
®Italy	1	Spain	0
Czechoslovakia	3	Switzerland	2

SEMI FINALS

Czechoslovakia	3	Germany	1
Italy	1	Austria	0

THIRD PLACE MATCH

Germany	3	Austria	2

FINAL - JUNE 10: FLAMINIO, ROME

Italy 2 (Orsi 81, Schiavio 95) **Czechoslovakia 1** (Puc 71)*

HT: 0-0. 90min: 1-1. Att: 55,000. Ref: Eklind (Sweden)

Italy: Combi - Monzeglio, Allemandi - Ferraris IV, Monti, Bertolini - Guaita, Meazza, Schiavio, Ferrari, Orsi.

Czechoslovakia: Planicka - Zenisek, Ctyroky - Kostalek, Cambal, Kreil - Junek, Svoboda, Sobotka, Nejedly, Puc.

Top scorers: 4 Nejedly (Czechoslovakia), Schiavio (Italy), Conen (Germany).

1938 FRANCE

The shadow of war hung over the 1938 finals in France. Argentina and Uruguay stayed away in anger at the event remaining in Europe, while Austria withdrew after the country was swallowed up into Hitler's Greater Germany. The football was equally tense. In the knock-out style first round, Hungary and France were the only teams to progress without needing extra time or replays. The most dramatic game saw Brazil beat Poland 6–5 after extra time in Strasbourg with centre-forwards Leonidas and Ernst Willimowski each scoring hat-tricks. Brazil then needed a replay to beat Czechoslovakia and earn a semi-final joust with Italy, whose captain Giuseppe Meazza converted the winning penalty. Hungary beat Sweden 5–1 in the other semi-final to earn the right to face Italy in the final in the Stade Colombes in Paris. Ruthless manager Vittorio Pozzo had retained only two of his 1934 winners in the shape of inside forward Meazza and Gioanin Ferrari. But Italy had few problems retaining the cup. Gino Colaussi and Silvio Piola each scored twice in a 4–2 win.

FIRST ROUND

* After extra time ® Replay

Switzerland	1	Germany	1*
Switzerland	4	Germany	2®
Cuba	3	Romania	3*
Cuba	2	Romania	1®
Hungary	6	Dutch East Indies	0
France	3	Belgium	1
Czechoslovakia	3	Holland	0*
Brazil	6	Poland	5*
Italy	2	Norway	1*

SECOND ROUND

Sweden	8	Cuba	0
Hungary	2	Switzerland	0
Italy	3	France	1
Brazil	1	Czechoslovakia	1*
Brazil	2	Czechoslovakia	1®

SEMI FINALS

Italy	2	Brazil	1
Hungary	5	Sweden	1

THIRD PLACE MATCH

Brazil	4	Sweden	2

FINAL - JUNE 19: COLOMBES, PARIS

Italy 4 (Colaussi 5, 35, Piola 16, 82) **Hungary 2** (Titkos 7, Sarosi 70)

HT: 3-1. Att: 55,000. Ref: Capdeville (France)

Italy: Olivieri - Foni, Andreolo, Rava - Serantoni, Locatelli - Biavati, Meazza, Piola, Ferrari, Colaussi.

Hungary: Szabo - Polgar, Biro - Szalay, Szucs, Lazar - Sas, Vincze, Sarosi, Szengeller, Titkos.

Top scorer: 8 Leonidas (Brazil); 7 Szengeller (Hungary); 5 Piola (Italy).

1950 BRAZIL

The finals in Brazil were marked by two of the greatest shocks in the history of the World Cup. Joint favourites before kick-off were the hosts and the old masters from England, competing for the first time. Brazil at least reached the final but England did not progress beyond the first round group stage after a humiliating 1–0 defeat by a scratch team from the United States. Holders Italy also crashed out in the first round, having failed to recover from the effects of the Torino air disaster a year earlier in which 10 Italian internationals had been killed. There was no formal final for the one and only time. Brazil, Uruguay, Sweden and Spain qualified for a final group in which the hosts walked out to face Uruguay in the last match needing only a draw to win the World Cup. Uruguay had to win. Almost 200,000 delirious fans jammed Rio's Maracana stadium but by the final whistle they had been plunged into depression after the visitors hit back from 1–0 down to win 2–1. After 20 years, and against all the odds, the Cup had returned to Uruguay.

POOL 1

Brazil	4	Mexico	0
Yugoslavia	3	Switzerland	0
Yugoslavia	4	Mexico	1
Brazil	2	Switzerland	2
Brazil	2	Yugoslavia	0
Switzerland	2	Mexico	1

	P	W	D	L	F	A	Pts
Brazil	3	3	1	0	8	2	5
Yugoslavia	3	2	0	1	7	3	4
Switzerland	3	1	1	1	4	6	3
Mexico	3	0	0	3	2	10	0

POOL 2

Spain	3	USA	1
England	2	Chile	0
USA	1	England	0
Spain	2	Chile	0
Spain	1	England	0
Chile	5	USA	2

	P	W	D	L	F	A	Pts
Spain	3	3	0	0	6	1	6
England	3	1	0	2	2	2	2
Chile	3	1	0	2	5	6	2
USA	3	1	0	2	4	8	2

POOL 3

Sweden	3	Italy	2
Sweden	2	Paraguay	2
Italy	2	Paraguay	0

	P	W	D	L	F	A	Pts
Sweden	2	1	1	0	5	4	3
Italy	2	1	0	1	4	3	2
Paraguay	2	0	1	1	2	4	1

POOL 4

Uruguay	8	Bolivia	0

	P	W	D	L	F	A	Pts
Uruguay	1	1	0	0	8	0	2
Bolivia	1	0	0	1	0	8	0

FINAL POOL

Uruguay	2	Spain	2
Brazil	7	Sweden	1
Uruguay	3	Sweden	2
Brazil	6	Spain	1
Sweden	3	Spain	1
Uruguay	2	Brazil	1

	P	W	D	L	F	A	Pts
Uruguay	3	2	1	0	7	5	5
Brazil	3	2	0	1	14	4	4
Sweden	3	1	0	2	6	11	2
Spain	3	0	1	2	4	11	1

FINAL - JULY 16: MARACANA, RIO DE JANEIRO

Brazil 1 (Friaca 47) **Uruguay 2** (Schiaffino 66, Ghiggia 79)

HT: 0–0. Att: 199,000. Ref: Reader (England)

Brazil: Barbosa - Da Costa, Juvenal - Bauer, Alvim, Bigode - Friaca, Zizinho, Ademir, Jair, Chico.

Uruguay: Maspoli - Gonzales, Tejera - Gambetta, Varela, Andrade - Ghiggia, Perez, Miguez, Schiaffino, Moran.

Top scorer: Top scorer: 7 Ademir (Brazil)

1954 SWITZERLAND

The magic of Ferenc Puskas and Sandor Kocsis meant Hungary were hottest-ever favourites on their arrival in FIFA's own back yard in Switzerland. They were Olympic champions, had inflicted England's first home defeat by continental opposition and fired 17 goals in their opening two group matches against South Korea and West Germany. But no-one could know the significance of the ankle injury inflicted on Puskas by a heavy tackle from German defender Werner Liebrich. Without their captain, Hungary outfought

POOL 1

Yugoslavia	1	France	0
Brazil	5	Mexico	0
France	3	Mexico	2
Brazil	1	Yugoslavia	1

	P	W	D	L	F	A	Pts
Brazil	2	1	1	0	6	1	3
Yugoslavia	2	1	1	0	2	1	3
France	2	1	0	1	3	3	2
Mexico	2	0	0	2	2	8	0

POOL 2

Hungary	9	Korea	0
West Germany	4	Turkey	1
Hungary	8	West Germany	3
Turkey	7	Korea	0

	P	W	D	L	F	A	Pts
Hungary	2	2	0	0	17	3	4
West Germany	2	1	0	1	7	9	2
Turkey	2	1	0	1	8	4	2
Korea	2	0	0	2	0	16	0

Brazil 4–2 in a quarter-final dubbed the "Battle of Bern", then defeated holders Uruguay 4–2 in a wonderful semi-final. The Uruguayans had previously beaten an England side boasting 39-year-old Stanley Matthews. Hungary gambled on recalling Puskas for the final repeat against the Germans. He scored an early goal as Hungary raced to 2–0 ahead but his lack of fitness proved a crucial handicap in the closing stages when Germany battled back to win 3–2. Hungary, unbeaten in four years, had lost the one match which mattered most.

POOL 3

Austria	1	Scotland	0
Uruguay	2	Czechoslovakia	0
Austria	5	Czechoslovakia	0
Uruguay	7	Scotland	0

	P	W	D	L	F	A	Pts
Uruguay	2	2	0	0	9	0	4
Austria	2	2	0	0	6	0	4
Czechoslovakia	2	0	0	2	0	7	0
Scotland	2	0	0	2	0	8	0

POOL 4

England	4	Belgium	4
England	2	Switzerland	0
Switzerland	2	Italy	1
Italy	4	Belgium	1

	P	W	D	L	F	A	Pts
England	2	1	1	0	6	4	3
Italy	2	1	0	1	5	3	2
Switzerland	2	1	0	1	2	3	2
Belgium	2	0	1	1	5	8	1

PLAY OFF

Switzerland	4	Italy	1

QUARTER FINALS

West Germany	2	Yugoslavia	0
Hungary	4	Brazil	2
Austria	7	Switzerland	5
Uruguay	4	England	2

SEMI FINALS

West Germany	6	Austria	1
Hungary	4	Uruguay	2

THIRD-PLACE MATCH

Austria	3	Uruguay	1

FINAL – JULY 4: WANKDORF, BERN

West Germany 3 (Morlock 10, Rahn 18, 82) **Hungary 2** (Puskas 6, Czibor 8)
HT: 2–2. Att: 60,000. Ref: Ling (England)
West Germany: Turek - Posipal, Liebrich, Kohlmeyer - Eckel, Mai - Rahn, Morlock, O Walter, F Walter, Schafer.
Hungary: Grosics - Buzansky, Lorant, Lantos - Bozsik, Zakarias - Czibor, Kocsis, Hidegkuti, Puskas, M Toth.
Top scorer: 11 Kocsis (Hungary)

1958 SWEDEN

Brazil became the first nation to win the World Cup on the "wrong" continent after introducing the world to the outstanding individual talents of Didi, Garrincha and Pele, as well as a revolutionary tactical formation known as 4-2-4. They thrashed hosts Sweden 5–2 in the final in Stockholm. France finished a best-yet third thanks to the record-breaking marksmanship of centre-forward Just Fontaine who scored 13 goals, including four in the third-place victory over deposed champions West Germany. For the only time, all four British home nations reached the finals. Wales and Northern Ireland reached the quarter-finals but England and Scotland fell in the group stage. England, weakened by the Munich air crash deaths of Manchester United players including Duncan Edwards, lost a first-round play-off to World Cup newcomers from the Soviet Union. Pele, 17, missed the Brazilians' opening two matches through injury but ended with six goals including a semi-final hat-trick against France and two more in the final against the Swedes.

POOL 1

W.Germany	3	Argentina	1
Northern Ireland	1	Czechoslovakia	0
W.Germany	2	Czechoslovakia	2
Argentina	3	Northern Ireland	1
West Germany	2	Northern Ireland	2
Czechoslovakia	6	Argentina	1

	P	W	D	L	F	A	Pts
West Germany	3	1	2	0	7	5	4
Czechoslovakia	3	1	1	1	8	4	3
Northern Ireland	3	1	0	1	4	5	3
Argentina	3	1	0	2	5	10	2

POOL 2

France	7	Paraguay	3
Yugoslavia	1	Scotland	1
Yugoslavia	3	France	2
Paraguay	3	Scotland	2
France	2	Scotland	1
Yugoslavia	3	Paraguay	3

	P	W	D	L	F	A	Pts
France	3	2	0	1	11	7	4
Yugoslavia	3	1	2	0	7	6	4
Pararguay	3	1	1	1	9	12	3
Scotland	3	0	1	2	4	6	1

POOL 3

Sweden	3	Mexico	0
Hungary	1	Wales	1
Wales	1	Mexico	1
Sweden	2	Hungary	1
Sweden	0	Wales	0
Hungary	4	Mexico	0

	P	W	D	L	F	A	Pts
Sweden	3	2	1	0	5	1	5
Hungary	3	1	1	1	6	3	3
Wales	3	0	3	0	2	2	3
Mexico	3	0	1	2	1	8	1

POOL 4

England	2	Soviet Union	2
Brazil	3	Austria	0
England	0	Brazil	0
Soviet Union	2	Austria	0
Brazil	2	Soviet Union	0
England	2	Austria	2

	P	W	D	L	F	A	Pts
Brazil	3	2	1	0	5	0	5
England	3	0	3	0	4	4	3
Soviet Union	3	1	1	1	4	4	3
Austria	3	0	1	2	2	7	1

PLAY OFFS

Northern Ireland	2	Czechoslovakia	1
Wales	2	Hungary	1
Soviet Union	1	England	0

QUARTER FINALS

France	4	Northern Ireland	0
West Germany	1	Yugoslavia	0
Sweden	2	Soviet Union	0
Brazil	1	Wales	0

SEMI FINALS

Brazil	5	France	2
Sweden	3	West Germany	1

THIRD-PLACE MATCH

France	6	West Germany	3

FINAL – JUNE 29: RASUNDA, STOCKHOLM

Brazil 5 (Vava 9, 30, Pele 55, 90, Zagalo 68) **Sweden 2** (Liedholm 4, Simonsson 80)
HT: 2–1. Att: 49,737. Ref: Guigue (France)
Brazil: Gilmar – D Santos, Bellini, Orlando, N Santos – Zito, Didi - Garrincha, Vava, Pele, Zagalo.
Sweden: Svensson - Bergmark, Gustavsson, Axbom - Borjesson, Parling - Hamrin, Gren, Simonsson, Liedholm, Skoglund.
Top scorer: 13 Fontaine (France)

1962 CHILE

Brazil retained their world crown despite losing Pele, now indisputably the world's finest player, to injury after only two matches. The holders amply compensated for both his loss and the ageing of their team by converting their 4-2-4 system into a more cautious 4-3-3. The bow-legged Garrincha took centre stage in Pele's absence, scoring twice in both the quarter-finals against England and the semi-final against hosts Chile. The "Little Bird" was also sent off against the Chileans but was cleared for the final in which Brazil beat Czechoslovakia 3-1. The Czechs succumbed after taking the lead through playmaker Jozef Masopust whose consolation prize was to be hailed as European Footballer of the Year. The finals were marred, however, by violence – most infamously in the "Battle of Santiago" between Chile and Italy. Two Italians were sent off by English referee Ken Aston who somehow missed the flagrant, flailing left hook with which Chile's Leonel Sanchez broke the nose of Italy's Humberto Maschio.

GROUP 1

Uruguay	2	Colombia	1
Soviet Union	2	Yugoslavia	0
Yugoslavia	3	Uruguay	1
Soviet Union	4	Colombia	4
Soviet Union	2	Uruguay	1
Yugoslavia	5	Colombia	0

	P	W	D	L	F	A	Pts
Soviet Union	3	2	1	0	8	5	5
Yugoslavia	3	2	0	1	8	3	4
Uruguay	3	1	0	2	4	6	2
Colombia	3	0	1	2	25	11	1

GROUP 2

Chile	3	Switzerland	1
West Germany	0	Italy	0
Chile	2	Italy	0
West Germany	2	Switzerland	1
West Germany	2	Chile	0
Italy	3	Switzerland	0

	P	W	D	L	F	A	Pts
West Germany	3	2	1	0	4	1	5
Chile	3	2	0	1	5	3	4
Italy	3	1	1	1	3	2	3
Switzerland	3	0	0	3	2	8	0

GROUP 3

Brazil	2	Mexico	0
Czechoslovakia	1	Spain	0
Brazil	0	Czechoslovakia	0
Spain	1	Mexico	0
Brazil	2	Spain	1
Mexico	3	Czechoslovakia	1

	P	W	D	L	F	A	Pts
Brazil	3	2	1	0	4	1	5
Czechoslovakia	3	1	1	1	2	3	3
Mexico	3	1	0	2	2	3	2
Spain	3	1	0	2	2	3	2

GROUP 4

Argentina	1	Bulgaria	0
Hungary	2	England	1
England	3	Argentina	1
Hungary	6	Bulgaria	1
Argentina	0	Hungary	0
England	0	Bulgaria	0

	P	W	D	L	F	A	Pts
Hungary	3	2	1	0	8	2	5
England	3	1	1	1	4	3	3
Argentina	3	1	1	1	2	3	3
Bulgaria	3	0	1	2	1	7	1

QUARTER-FINALS

Yugoslavia	1	West Germany	0
Brazil	3	England	1
Chile	2	Soviet Union	1
Czechoslovakia	1	Hungary	0

SEMI-FINALS

Brazil	4	Chile	2
Czechoslovakia	3	Yugoslavia	1

FINAL — JUNE 17: NACIONAL, SANTIAGO

Brazil 3 (Amarildo 18, Zito 69, Vava 77) **Czechoslovakia 1** (Masopust 16)
HT: 1-1. Att: 68,679. Ref: Latishev (Soviet Union)
Brazil: Gilmar – D Santos, Mauro, Zozimo, N Santos - Zito, Didi, Zagallo - Garrincha, Vava, Amarildo.
Czechoslovakia: Schroiff - Tichy, Pluskal, Popluhar, Novak – Kvasniak, Kadraba, Masopust - Pospichal, Scherer, Jelinek.
Top scorer: 4 Garrincha (Brazil), Vava (Brazil), L Sanchez (Chile), Jerkovic (Yugoslavia), Albert (Hungary), V Ivanov Sov).

THIRD PLACE MATCH

Chile	1	Yugoslavia	0

1966 ENGLAND

England, home of the game, celebrated the nation's only World Cup triumph after a tournament rich in drama. The hosts provided some, though not all, through the contrasts of a bad-tempered quarter-final defeat of Argentina, a classic semi-final defeat of Portugal and a controversial 4–2 extra-time triumph over West Germany in the final. The Queen was in the crowd to see Geoff Hurst become the only player in World Cup history to score a final hat-trick including a controversial second which may, or may not, have crossed the goal-line. England's explosive Bobby Charlton, West Germany's graceful young Franz Beckenbauer and Portugal's thunderous Eusebio, the tournament's nine-goal top scorer, took individual honours. The mystery men from North Korea provided the greatest upset, defeating mighty Italy in the first round with a goal from dentist-turned-inside-forward Pak Do Ik. Brazil, too old for the challenge this time around, limped home in great disappointment after being kicked to first-round elimination.

GROUP 1

England	0	Uruguay	0
France	1	Mexico	1
Uruguay	2	France	1
England	2	Mexico	0
Uruguay	0	Mexico	0
England	2	France	0

	P	W	D	L	F	A	Pts
England	3	2	1	0	4	0	5
Uruguay	3	1	2	0	2	1	4
Mexico	3	1	2	1	1	3	2
France	3	0	1	2	2	5	1

GROUP 2

West Germany	5	Switzerland	0
Argentina	2	Spain	1
Spain	2	Switzerland	1
Argentina	0	West Germany	0
Argentina	2	Switzerland	0
West Germany	2	Spain	1

	P	W	D	L	F	A	Pts
West Germany	3	2	1	0	7	1	5
Argentina	3	2	1	0	4	1	5
Spain	3	1	0	2	4	5	2
Switzerland	3	0	0	3	1	9	0

GROUP 3

Brazil	2	Bulgaria	0
Portugal	3	Hungary	1
Hungary	3	Brazil	1
Portugal	3	Bulgaria	0
Portugal	3	Brazil	1
Hungary	3	Bulgaria	1

	P	W	D	L	F	A	Pts
Portugal	3	3	0	0	9	2	6
Hungary	3	2	0	1	7	5	4
Brazil	3	1	0	2	4	6	2
Bulgaria	3	0	0	3	1	8	0

GROUP 4

Soviet Union	3	North Korea	0
Italy	2	Chile	0
Chile	1	North Korea	1
Soviet Union	1	Italy	0
North Korea	1	Italy	0
Soviet Union	2	Chile	1

	P	W	D	L	F	A	Pts
Soviet Union	3	3	0	0	6	1	6
North Korea	3	1	1	1	2	4	3
Italy	3	1	0	2	2	2	2
Chile	3	0	1	2	2	5	1

QUARTER FINALS

England	1	Argentina	0
West Germany	4	Uruguay	0
Portugal	5	North Korea	3
Soviet Union	2	Hungary	1

SEMI FINALS

West Germany	2	Soviet Union	1
England	2	Portugal	1

THIRD-PLACE MATCH

Portugal	2	Soviet Union	1

FINAL — JULY 30: WEMBLEY

* After extra time

***England 4** (Hurst 19, 100, 120, Peters 77) **West Germany 2** (Haller 13, Weber 89)
HT: 1-1. 90min: 2-2. Att: 96,924. Ref: Dienst (Switzerland)
England: Banks - Cohen, J Charlton, Moore, Wilson - Ball, Stiles, R Charlton, Peters - Hurst, Hunt.
West Germany: Tilkowski - Hottges, Schulz, Weber, Schnellinger - Haller, Beckenbauer, Overath - Seeler, Held, Emmerich.
Top scorer: 9 Eusebio (Portugal).

1970 MEXICO

The heat and altitude of Mexico enforced a slower rhythm on the finals which resulted in some of the most skilful football seen thus far in the World Cup. Brazil, rebuilt around a revived Pele, revelled in the conditions. Jairzinho – the right-wing heir to Garrincha – made individual history by scoring in all their seven matches up to and including the classic 4–1 final thrashing of Italy in Mexico City's Azteca stadium. Fatigue, as well as Brazilian verve, got the better of an Italian side who had barely recovered from a dramatic 4–3 extra-time victory over West Germany in the semi-finals. The Germans, inspired by a new goal machine in Gerd Muller, had hardly caught their breath themselves after a thrilling 3–2 comeback victory over outgoing champions England in the quarter-finals. England had badly missed World Cup-winning goalkeeping hero Gordon Banks, ruled out by illness. He had been one of the stars of the first round, courtesy of an amazing save from Pele in a group game against Brazil.

GROUP 1

Mexico	0	Soviet Union	0
Belgium	3	El Salvador	0
Soviet Union	4	Belgium	1
Mexico	4	El Salvador	0
Soviet Union	2	El Salvador	0
Mexico	1	Belgium	0

	P	W	D	L	F	A	Pts
Soviet Union	3	2	1	0	6	1	5
Mexico	3	2	1	0	5	0	5
Belgium	3	1	0	2	4	5	2
El Salvador	3	0	0	3	0	9	0

GROUP 2

Uruguay	2	Israel	0
Italy	1	Sweden	0
Uruguay	0	Italy	0
Sweden	1	Israel	1
Sweden	1	Uruguay	0
Italy	0	Israel	0

	P	W	D	L	F	A	Pts
Italy	3	1	2	0	1	0	4
Uruguay	3	1	1	1	2	1	3
Sweden	3	1	1	1	2	2	3
Israel	3	0	2	1	1	3	2

GROUP 3

England	1	Romania	0
Brazil	4	Czechoslovakia	1
Romania	2	Czechoslovakia	1
Brazil	1	England	0
Brazil	3	Romania	2
England	1	Czechoslovakia	0

	P	W	D	L	F	A	Pts
Brazil	3	3	0	0	8	3	6
England	3	2	0	1	2	1	4
Romania	3	1	0	2	4	5	2
Czechoslovakia	3	0	0	3	2	7	0

GROUP 4

Peru	3	Bulgaria	2
West Germany	2	Morocco	1
Peru	3	Morocco	0
West Germany	5	Bulgaria	2
West Germany	3	Peru	1
Morocco	1	Bulgaria	1

	P	W	D	L	F	A	Pts
West Germany	3	3	0	0	10	4	6
Peru	3	2	0	1	7	5	4
Bulgaria	3	0	1	2	5	9	1
Morocco	3	0	1	2	2	6	1

QUARTER-FINALS

* After extra time

West Germany	3	England	2*
Brazil	4	Peru	2
Italy	4	Mexico	1
Uruguay	1	Soviet Union	0

SEMI-FINALS

* After extra time

Italy	4	West Germany	3*
Brazil	3	Uruguay	1

THIRD PLACE MATCH

West Germany	1	Uruguay	0

FINAL — JUNE 21: AZTECA, MEXICO CITY

Brazil 4 (Pele 18, Gerson 66, Jairzinho 71, Carlos Alberto 86) **Italy 1** (Boninsegna 37)
HT: 1-1. Att: 107,000. Ref: Glockner (East Germany)
Brazil: Felix - Carlos Alberto, Brito, Piazza, Everaldo - Clodoaldo, Gerson, Rivelino - Jairzinho, Tostao, Pele.
Italy: Albertosi – Facchetti - Cera, Burgnich, Rosato – Domenghini, Bertini (Juliano 75), De Sisti – Mazzola - Boninsegna (Rivera 84), Riva.
Top scorer: 9 Müller (West Germany).

1974 WEST GERMANY

West Germany's Bayern Munich had just taken over from Holland's Ajax Amsterdam as Europe's top club and that tilt in the balance of power was repeated at national team level. The Dutch played the finest football of the finals as their "total football" swirled them to the final in Munich. But despite going head inside two minutes with the first-ever final penalty – converted by Johan Neeskens – they lost 2–1. Their captain and inspiration Johan Cruyff wasted too much of his energy

FIRST ROUND - GROUP 1

West Germany	1	Chile	0
East Germany	2	Australia	0
West Germany	3	Australia	0
East Germany	1	Chile	1
East Germany	1	West Germany	0
Chile	0	Australia	0

	P	W	D	L	F	A	Pts
West Germany	3	2	1	0	4	1	5
East Germany	3	2	0	1	4	1	4
Chile	3	0	2	1	1	2	1
Australia	3	0	1	2	0	5	1

FIRST ROUND - GROUP 2

Brazil	0	Yugoslavia	0
Scotland	2	Zaïre	0
Brazil	0	Scotland	0
Yugoslavia	9	Zaïre	0
Scotland	1	Yugoslavia	1
Brazil	3	Zaïre	0

	P	W	D	L	F	A	Pts
Yugoslavia	3	1	2	0	10	1	4
Brazil	3	1	2	0	3	0	4
Scotland	3	1	2	0	3	1	4
Zaïre	3	0	0	3	0	14	0

arguing over decisions with English referee Jack Taylor. No fewer than six Bayern players, headed by skipper and attacking sweeper Franz Beckenbauer, laid their hands on the World Cup in their own, home stadium. Earlier the hosts had lost a group game to their cousins from communist East Germany, while Brazil had been dethroned by the Dutch. Olympic champions Poland, surprise victors over England in the qualifying competition, finished third. Striker Grzegorz Lato was the tournament's seven-goal top scorer.

FIRST ROUND - GROUP 3

Holland	2	Uruguay	0
Sweden	0	Bulgaria	0
Holland	0	Sweden	0
Bulgaria	1	Uruguay	1
Holland	4	Bulgaria	1
Sweden	3	Uruguay	0

	P	W	D	L	F	A	Pts
Holland	3	2	1	0	6	1	5
Sweden	3	1	2	0	3	0	4
Bulgaria	3	0	2	1	2	5	2
Uruguay	3	0	1	2	1	6	1

FIRST ROUND - POOL 4

Italy	3	Haiti	1
Poland	3	Argentina	2
Italy	1	Argentina	1
Poland	7	Haiti	0
Argentina	4	Haiti	1
Poland	2	Italy	1

	P	W	D	L	F	A	Pts
Poland	3	3	0	0	0	3	6
Argentina	3	1	1	1	1	5	3
Italy	3	1	1	1	1	4	3
Haiti	3	0	0	0	3	14	0

SECOND ROUND - GROUP A

Brazil	1	East Germany	0
Holland	4	Argentina	0
Holland	2	East Germany	0
Brazil	2	Argentina	1
Holland	2	Brazil	0
Argentina	1	East Germany	1

	P	W	D	L	F	A	Pts
Holland	3	3	0	0	8	0	6
Brazil	3	2	0	1	3	3	4
East Germany	3	0	1	2	1	4	1
Argentina	3	0	1	2	2	7	1

SECOND ROUND - GROUP B

Poland	1	Sweden	0
West Germany	2	Yugoslavia	0
Poland	2	Yugoslavia	1
West Germany	4	Sweden	2
Sweden	2	Yugoslavia	1
West Germany	1	Poland	0

	P	W	D	L	F	A	Pts
West Germany	3	3	0	0	7	2	6
Poland	3	2	0	1	3	2	4
Sweden	3	1	0	2	4	6	2
Yugoslavia	3	0	0	3	2	6	0

THIRD-PLACE MATCH

Poland	1	Brazil	0

FINAL — JULY 7: OLYMPIA, MUNICH

West Germany 2 (Breitner 25 pen, Muller 43)
Holland 1 (Neeskens 2 pen)
HT: 2-1. Att: 77,833. Ref: Taylor (England)
West Germany: Maier - Vogts, Schwarzenbeck, Beckenbauer, Breitner - Bonhof, Hoeness, Overath - Grabowski, Muller, Holzenbein.
Holland: Jongbloed - Suurbier, Rijsbergen (De Jong 69), Haan, Krol - Jansen, Neeskens, Van Hanegem – Cruyff - Rep, Rensenbrink (R Van de Kerkhof 46).
Top scorer: 7 Lato (Poland).

1978 ARGENTINA

Argentina very nearly did not host the World Cup. It took enormous investment from the military junta to bring infrastructure and organisation up to speed amid worldwide controversy over the country's sinister policy of political repression. Perhaps to try to blot out all that, the Argentine nation thrilled to their team's first-ever World Cup win. Manager Cesar Menotti left out the precocious teenager Diego Maradona in favour of just one foreign-based player. But that player, the Valencia striker Mario Kempes, proved the tournament's outstanding individual. He top-scored with six goals including two in the extra-time defeat of Holland – runners-up again – in the final. Holders West Germany faded away in the second round, while Brazil finished third. Scotland were British football's sole representatives. They fell in the first round where delight over a "goal of the tournament" by Archie Gemmill against Holland was balanced by the embarrassment of winger Willie Johnston being sent home after becoming the first dope-test failure at a World Cup.

FIRST ROUND - GROUP 1

Argentina	2	Hungary	1
Italy	2	France	1
Argentina	2	France	1
Italy	3	Hungary	1
Italy	1	Argentina	0
France	3	Hungary	1

	P	W	D	L	F	A	Pts
Italy	3	3	0	0	6	2	6
Argentina	3	2	0	1	4	3	4
France	3	1	0	2	5	5	2
Hungary	3	0	0	3	3	8	0

FIRST ROUND - GROUP 2

West Germany	0	Poland	0
Tunisia	3	Mexico	1
Poland	1	Tunisia	0
West Germany	6	Mexico	0
Poland	3	Mexico	1
West Germany	0	Tunisia	0

	P	W	D	L	F	A	Pts
Poland	3	2	1	0	4	1	5
West Germany	3	1	2	0	6	0	4
Tunisia	3	1	1	1	3	2	3
Mexico	3	0	0	3	2	12	0

FIRST ROUND - GROUP 3

Austria	2	Spain	1
Sweden	1	Brazil	1
Austria	1	Sweden	0
Brazil	0	Spain	0
Spain	1	Sweden	0
Brazil	1	Austria	0

	P	W	D	L	F	A	Pts
Austria	3	2	1	0	6	1	5
Brazil	3	1	2	0	3	0	4
Spain	3	0	2	1	2	5	2
Sweden	3	0	1	2	1	6	1

FIRST ROUND - GROUP 4

Peru	3	Scotland	1
Holland	3	Iran	1
Scotland	1	Iran	1
Holland	0	Peru	0
Peru	4	Iran	1
Scotland	3	Holland	2

	P	W	D	L	F	A	Pts
Peru	3	2	1	0	7	2	5
Holland	3	1	1	1	5	3	3
Scotland	3	1	1	1	5	6	3
Iran	3	0	1	2	2	8	1

SECOND ROUND - GROUP A

Italy	0	West Germany	0
Holland	5	Austria	1
Italy	1	Austria	0
Austria	3	West Germany	2
Holland	2	Italy	1
Holland	2	West Germany	2

	P	W	D	L	F	A	Pts
Holland	3	2	1	0	9	4	5
Italy	3	1	1	1	2	2	3
West Germany	3	0	2	1	4	5	2
Austria	3	1	0	2	4	8	2

SECOND ROUND - GROUP B

Argentina	2	Poland	0
Brazil	3	Peru	0
Argentina	0	Brazil	0
Poland	1	Peru	0
Brazil	3	Poland	1
Argentina	6	Peru	0

	P	W	D	L	F	A	Pts
Argentina	3	2	1	0	8	0	5
Brazil	3	2	1	0	6	1	5
Poland	3	1	0	2	2	5	2
Peru	3	0	0	3	0	10	0

THIRD-PLACE MATCH

Poland	1	Brazil	0

FINAL — JUNE 25: MONUMENTAL, BUENOS AIRES

* After extra time

***Argentina 3** (Kempes 37, 104, Bertoni 114)
Holland 1 (Nanninga 81)
HT: 1-0. 90min: 1-1. Att: 77,260. Ref: Gonella (Italy)
Argentina: Fillol - Olguin, Galvan, Passarella, Tarantini - Ardiles (Larrosa 66), Gallego - Bertoni, Kempes, Ortiz (Houseman 75) - Luque.
Holland: Jongbloed - Krol, Poortvliet, Brandts, Jansen (Suurbier 73) – R Van de Kerkhof, Neeskens, W Van de Kerkhof, Haan - Rep (Nanninga 59), Rensenbrink.
Top scorer: 6 Kempes (Argentina).

FIRST ROUND - GROUP 1

Italy	0	Poland	0
Peru	0	Cameroon	0
Italy	1	Peru	1
Poland	0	Cameroon	0
Poland	5	Peru	1
Italy	1	Cameroon	1

	P	W	D	L	F	A	Pts
Poland	3	1	2	0	5	1	4
Italy	3	0	3	0	2	2	3
Cameroon	3	0	3	0	1	1	3
Peru	3	0	2	1	2	6	2

FIRST ROUND - GROUP 2

Algeria	2	West Germany	1
Austria	1	Chile	0
West Germany	4	Chile	1
Austria	2	Algeria	1
Algeria	3	Chile	2
West Germany	1	Austria	0

	P	W	D	L	F	A	Pts
West Germany	3	2	0	1	6	3	4
Austria	3	2	0	1	3	1	4
Algeria	3	2	0	1	5	8	4
Chile	3	0	0	3	3	5	0

FIRST ROUND - GROUP 3

Belgium	1	Argentina	0
Hungary	10	El Salvador	1
Argentina	4	Hungary	1
Belgium	1	El Salvador	0
Belgium	1	Hungary	1
Argentina	2	El Salvador	0

	P	W	D	L	F	A	Pts
Belgium	3	2	1	0	3	1	5
Argentina	3	2	0	1	6	2	4
Hungary	3	1	1	1	12	6	3
El Salvador	3	0	0	3	1	13	3

FIRST ROUND - GROUP 4

England	3	France	1
Czechoslovakia	1	Kuwait	1
England	2	Czechoslovakia	0
France	4	Kuwait	1
France	1	Czechoslovakia	1
England	1	Kuwait	0

	P	W	D	L	F	A	Pts
England	3	3	0	0	6	1	6
France	3	1	1	1	2	4	3
Czechoslovakia	3	1	0	2	2	2	2
Kuwait	3	0	1	2	2	5	1

FIRST ROUND - GROUP 5

Spain	1	Honduras	1
N. Ireland	0	Yugoslavia	0
Spain	2	Yugoslavia	1
N.Ireland	1	Honduras	1
Yugoslavia	1	Honduras	0
N.Ireland	1	Spain	0

	P	W	D	L	F	A	Pts
N. Ireland	3	1	2	0	2	1	4
Spain	3	1	1	1	3	3	3
Yugoslavia	3	1	1	1	2	2	3
Honduras	3	0	2	1	2	3	2

FIRST ROUND - GROUP 6

Brazil	2	Soviet Union	1
Scotland	5	New Zealand	2
Brazil	4	Scotland	1
Soviet Union	3	New Zealand	0
Scotland	2	Soviet Union	2
Brazil	4	New Zealand	0

	P	W	D	L	F	A	Pts
Brazil	3	3	0	0	10	2	6
Soviet Union	3	1	1	1	6	4	3
Scotland	3	1	1	1	8	8	3
New Zealand	3	0	0	3	2	12	0

1982 SPAIN

Italy emulated Brazil's World Cup hat-trick despite drawing all three of their first-round matches. Paolo Rossi was their unlikely hero. He top-scored with six goals, including a second round hat-trick to beat Brazil, despite having only just returned after an 18-month ban following a betting-and-bribes scandal. Italy also saw off holders Argentina whose new wonder boy, Diego Maradona, achieved only notoriety after being sent off in a defeat by Brazil. Hosts Spain were another disappointment, never recovering confidence or momentum after a surprise early defeat by Northern Ireland. The most memorable match was a semi-final in Seville in which West Germany beat France in a first finals shoot-out after a 3–3 extra-time draw. France's Michel Platini put in a man-of-the-match performance in vain. The Germans, undermined by the fragile fitness of skipper Karl-Heinz Rummenigge, progressed only to a 3–1 defeat in the final. Italy won a third cup despite seeing Antonio Cabrini commit a first-ever final failure from the penalty spot.

SECOND ROUND – GROUP A

Poland	3	Belgium	0
Soviet Union	1	Belgium	0
Soviet Union	0	Poland	0

	P	W	D	L	F	A	Pts
Poland	2	1	1	0	3	0	3
Soviet Union	2	1	1	0	1	0	3
Belgium	2	0	0	2	0	4	0

SECOND ROUND – GROUP B

West Germany	0	England	0
West Germany	2	Spain	1
England	0	Spain	0

	P	W	D	L	F	A	Pts
West Germany	2	1	1	0	2	1	3
England	2	0	2	0	0	0	2
Spain	2	0	1	1	1	2	1

SECOND ROUND – GROUP C

Italy	2	Argentina	1
Brazil	3	Argentina	1
Italy	3	Brazil	2

	P	W	D	L	F	A	Pts
Italy	2	2	0	0	5	3	4
Brazil	2	1	0	1	5	4	2
Argentina	2	0	0	2	2	5	0

SECOND ROUND – GROUP D

France	1	Austria	0
N.Ireland	2	Austria	2
France	4	N.Ireland	1

	P	W	D	L	F	A	Pts
France	2	2	0	0	5	1	4
Austria	2	0	1	1	2	3	1
N.Ireland	2	0	1	1	3	6	1

SEMI FINALS

* After extra time (pens)

Italy	2	Poland	0
West Germany	3 (5)	France	3* (4)

THIRD-PLACE MATCH

Poland	3	France	2

FINAL — JULY 11: BERNABEU, MADRID

Italy 3 (Rossi 56, Tardelli 69, Altobelli 80) **West Germany 1** (Breitner 82)
HT: 0-0. Att: 90,000. Ref: Coelho (Brazil)
Italy: Zoff – Scirea - Bergomi, Gentile, Collovati, Cabrini - Oriale, Tardelli - Conti, Graziani (Altobelli 8; Causio 88), Rossi.
West Germany: Schumacher - Kaltz, K Forster, Stielike, B Forster - Breitner, Dremmler (Hrubesch 63), Briegel - Littbarski, Fischer (H Muller 70), Rummenigge. **Top scorer:** 6 Rossi (Italy).

FIRST ROUND – GROUP A

Bulgaria	1	Italy	1
Argentina	3	South Korea	1
Italy	1	Argentina	1
Bulgaria	1	South Korea	1
Argentina	2	Bulgaria	0
Italy	3	South Korea	2

	P	W	D	L	F	A	Pts
Argentina	3	2	1	0	6	2	5
Italy	3	1	2	0	5	4	4
Bulgaria	3	0	2	1	2	4	2
South Korea	3	0	1	2	4	7	1

FIRST ROUND – GROUP B

Mexico	2	Belgium	1
Paraguay	1	Iraq	0
Mexico	1	Paraguay	1
Belgium	2	Iraq	1
Paraguay	2	Belgium	2
Mexico	1	Iraq	0

	P	W	D	L	F	A	Pts
Mexico	3	2	1	0	4	2	5
Paraguay	3	1	2	0	4	3	4
Belgium	3	1	1	1	5	5	4
Iraq	3	0	0	3	1	4	0

FIRST ROUND – GROUP C

Soviet Union	6	Hungary	0
France	1	Canada	0
Soviet Union	1	France	1
Hungary	2	Canada	0
France	3	Hungary	0
Soviet Union	2	Canada	0

	P	W	D	L	F	A	Pts
Soviet Union	3	2	1	0	9	1	5
France	3	2	1	0	5	1	5
Hungary	3	1	0	2	2	9	2
Canada	3	0	0	3	0	5	0

FIRST ROUND – GROUP D

Brazil	1	Spain	0
N.Ireland	1	Algeria	1
Spain	2	N.Ireland	1
Brazil	1	Algeria	0
Spain	3	Algeria	0
Brazil	3	N.Ireland	0

	P	W	D	L	F	A	Pts
Brazil	3	3	0	0	5	0	6
Spain	3	2	0	1	5	2	4
N.Ireland	3	0	1	2	2	6	1
Algeria	3	0	1	2	1	5	1

FIRST ROUND – GROUP E

West Germany	1	Uruguay	1
Denmark	1	Scotland	0
Denmark	6	Uruguay	1
West Germany	2	Scotland	1
Scotland	0	Uruguay	0
Denmark	2	West Germany	0

	P	W	D	L	F	A	Pts
Denmark	3	3	0	0	9	1	6
West Germany	3	1	1	1	3	4	3
Uruguay	3	0	2	1	2	7	2
Scotland	3	0	1	2	1	3	1

FIRST ROUND – GROUP F

Morocco	0	Poland	0
Portugal	1	England	0
England	0	Morocco	0
Poland	1	Portugal	0
England	3	Poland	0
Morocco	3	Portugal	1

	P	W	D	L	F	A	Pts
Morocco	3	1	2	0	3	1	4
England	3	1	1	1	3	1	3
Poland	3	1	1	1	1	3	3
Portugal	3	1	0	2	2	4	2

SECOND ROUND

* After extra time

Mexico	2	Bulgaria	0
Belgium	4	Soviet Union	3*
Brazil	4	Poland	0
Argentina	1	Uruguay	0
France	2	Italy	0
West Germany	1	Morocco	0
England	3	Paraguay	0
Spain	5	Denmark	1

QUARTER-FINALS

* After extra time

France	1	Brazil	1*
(France won 4–3 on pens)			
West Germany	0	Mexico	0*
(West Germany won 4–1 on pens)			
Argentina	2	England	1
Spain	1	Belgium	1*
(Belgium won 5–4 on pens)			

1986 MEXICO

Diego Maradona, for both good and ill, dominated Argentina's second World Cup triumph in three attempts. Now captain, he produced a series of inspirational displays worthy to rank alongside the likes of Pele. Even in the 3–2 final win over West Germany, when he had been largely marked out of the game by Lothar Matthaus, he found crucial time and space in the closing minutes to create the winner for Jorge Burruchaga. Maradona also scored two wonderful solo goals against England and Belgium but earned equal notoriety with his infamous "Hand of God" goal in the quarter-final defeat of the English. Brazil fell at the same stage on penalties against France for whom skipper Michel Platini marked his 31st birthday by scoring a goal in normal time but failing in the shoot-out. The French then subsided tamely in the semi-finals against a workmanlike West German side managed by their 1974 winning captain, Franz Beckenbauer. Mexico, late substitute hosts after Colombia pulled out, lost on penalties to Germany in the second round.

SEMI FINALS

Argentina	2	Belgium	0
West Germany	2	France	0

THIRD-PLACE MATCH

France	4	Belgium	2

FINAL — JUNE 29: AZTECA, MEXICO CITY

Argentina 3 (Brown 22, Valdano 56, Burruchaga 84) **West Germany 2** (Rummenigge 73, Völler 82)
HT: 1-0. Att: 114,590. Ref: Arppi Filho (Brazil)
Argentina: Pumpido - Cuciuffo, Brown, Ruggeri - Giusti, Burruchaga (Trobbiani 89), Batista, Enrique, Olarticoechea – Maradona, Valdano.
West Germany: Schumacher - Berthold, Jakobs, Forster, Eder, Brehme - Matthaus, Magath (D Hoeness 63), Briegel - Allofs (Voller 46), Rummenigge. **Top scorer:** 6 Lineker (England).

GROUP A

Italy	1	Austria	0
Czechoslovakia	5	USA	1
Italy	1	USA	0
Czechoslovakia	1	Austria	0
Italy	2	Czechoslovakia	0
Austria	2	USA	1

	P	W	D	L	F	A	Pts
Italy	3	3	2	0	4	0	6
Czechoslovakia	3	2	0	1	6	3	4
Austria	3	1	0	2	2	3	2
USA	3	0	0	3	2	8	0

GROUP B

Cameroon	1	Argentina	0
Romania	2	Soviet Union	0
Argentina	2	Soviet Union	0
Cameroon	2	Romania	1
Argentina	1	Romania	1
Soviet Union	4	Cameroon	0

	P	W	D	L	F	A	Pts
Cameroon	3	2	0	1	3	5	4
Romania	3	1	1	1	4	3	3
Argentina	3	1	1	1	3	2	3
Soviet Union	3	1	0	2	4	4	2

GROUP C

Brazil	2	Sweden	1
Costa Rica	1	Scotland	0
Brazil	1	Costa Rica	0
Scotland	2	Sweden	1
Brazil	1	Scotland	0
Costa Rica	2	Sweden	1

	P	W	D	L	F	A	Pts
Brazil	3	3	0	0	4	1	6
Costa Rica	3	2	0	1	3	2	4
Scotland	3	1	0	2	2	3	2
Sweden	3	0	0	3	3	6	0

1990 ITALY

GROUP D

Colombia	2	UAE	0
West Germany	4	Yugoslavia	1
Yugoslavia	1	Colombia	0
West Germany	5	UAE	1
West Germany	1	Colombia	1
Yugoslavia	4	UAE	1

	P	W	D	L	F	A	Pts
West Germany	3	2	1	0	10	3	5
Yugoslavia	3	2	0	1	6	5	4
Colombia	3	1	1	1	3	2	3
UAE	3	0	0	3	2	11	0

GROUP E

Belgium	2	South Korea	0
Uruguay	0	Spain	0
Belgium	3	Uruguay	1
Spain	3	South Korea	1
Spain	2	Belgium	1
Uruguay	1	South Korea	0

	P	W	D	L	F	A	Pts
Spain	3	2	1	0	5	2	5
Belgium	3	2	0	1	6	3	4
Uruguay	3	1	1	1	2	3	3
South Korea	3	0	0	3	1	6	0

GROUP F

England	1	Rep of Ireland	1
Holland	1	Egypt	1
England	0	Holland	0
Egypt	0	Rep of Ireland	0
England	1	Egypt	0
Holland	1	Rep of Ireland	1

	P	W	D	L	F	A	Pts
England	3	1	2	0	2	1	4
Rep of Ireland	3	0	3	0	2	2	3
Holland	3	0	3	0	2	2	3
Egypt	3	0	2	1	1	2	2

1990 ITALY

West Germany joined Brazil and Italy as hat-trick holders though the standard of football never matched the passionate enthusiasm of host Italy's fans. The shocks started immediately with newcomers Cameroon defeating holders Argentina 1-0 in the opening match. Argentina recovered to reach the final but Diego Maradona was restricted by a knee injury and they needed the penalty-defying heroics of goalkeeper Sergio Goycochea to see off Yugoslavia and Italy along the way. England marked their first return since 1970 by reaching the semi-finals. Germany, as in 1982 against France, again had the edge in the penalty shootout after a 1-1 draw. The Germans also won the final with a penalty, albeit in normal play, to beat Argentina 1-0 in Rome. Argentina, blaming defeat on everyone from FIFA president Joao Havelange down, finished with nine men. Pedro Monzon and Gustavo Dezotti were the first players ever sent off in a World Cup final. Franz Beckenbauer became the first man to both captain and then manage World Cup winners.

SECOND ROUND

* After extra time

Cameroon	2	Colombia	1*
Czechoslovakia	4	Costa Rica	1
Argentina	1	Brazil	0
West Germany	2	Holland	1
Rep of Ireland	0	Romania	0*
(Rep of Ireland won 5-4 on pens)			
Italy	2	Uruguay	0
Yugoslavia	2	Spain	1*
England	1	Belgium	0*

QUARTER-FINALS

* After extra time

Argentina	0	Yugoslavia	0*
(Argentina won 3-2 on pens)			
Italy	1	Rep of Ireland	0
West Germany	1	Czechoslovakia	0
England	3	Cameroon	2*

SEMI FINALS

Argentina	1	Italy	1*
(Argentina won 4-3 on pens)			
West Germany	1	England	1*
(West Germany won 4-3 on pens)			

THIRD-PLACE MATCH

Italy	2	England	1

FINAL — JULY 8: OLIMPICO, ROME

West Germany 1 (Brehme 84 pen) **Argentina 0**

HT: 0-0. Att: 73,603. Ref: Codesal (Mexico)

West Germany: Illgner - Berthold (Reuter 74), Kohler, Augenthaler, Brehme – Hassler, Buchwald, Matthaus - Littbarski, Voller, Klinsmann.

Argentina: Goycochea - Lorenzo, Ruggeri (Monzon 46), Serrizuela, Sensini - Simon, Basualdo, Burruchaga (Calderon 53) - Maradona, Troglio, Dezotti. **Sent off:** Monzon, Dezotti. **Top scorer:** 6 Schillaci (Italy).

GROUP A

USA	1	Switzerland	1
Colombia	1	Romania	3
USA	2	Colombia	1
Romania	1	Switzerland	4
USA	0	Romania	1
Switzerland	0	Colombia	2

	P	W	D	L	F	A	Pts
Romania	3	2	0	1	5	5	6
Switzerland	3	1	1	1	5	4	4
USA	3	1	1	1	3	3	4
Colombia	3	1	0	2	4	5	3

GROUP B

Cameroon	2	Sweden	2
Brazil	2	Russia	0
Brazil	3	Cameroon	0
Sweden	3	Russia	1
Russia	6	Cameroon	1
Brazil	1	Sweden	1

	P	W	D	L	F	A	Pts
Brazil	3	2	1	0	6	1	7
Sweden	3	1	2	0	6	4	5
Russia	3	1	0	2	7	6	3
Cameroon	3	0	1	2	3	11	1

GROUP C

Germany	1	Bolivia	0
Spain	2	South Korea	2
Germany	1	Spain	1
South Korea	0	Bolivia	0
Bolivia	1	Spain	3
Germany	3	South Korea	2

	P	W	D	L	F	A	Pts
Germany	3	2	1	0	5	3	7
Spain	3	1	2	0	6	4	5
South Korea	3	0	2	1	4	5	2
Bolivia	3	0	1	2	1	4	1

GROUP D

Argentina	4	Greece	0
Nigeria	3	Bulgaria	0
Argentina	2	Nigeria	1
Bulgaria	4	Greece	0
Greece	0	Nigeria	2
Argentina	0	Bulgaria	2

	P	W	D	L	F	A	Pts
Nigeria	3	2	0	1	6	2	6
Bulgaria	3	2	0	1	6	3	6
Argentina	3	2	0	1	6	3	6
Greece	3	0	0	3	0	10	1

GROUP E

Italy	0	Rep of Ireland	1
Norway	1	Mexico	0
Italy	1	Norway	0
Mexico	2	Rep of Ireland	1
Rep of Ireland	0	Norway	0
Italy	1	Mexico	1

	P	W	D	L	F	A	Pts
Mexico	3	1	1	1	3	3	4
Rep of Ireland	3	1	1	1	2	2	4
Italy	3	1	1	1	2	2	4
Norway	3	1	1	1	1	1	4

GROUP F

Belgium	1	Morocco	0
Holland	2	Saudi Arabia	1
Belgium	1	Holland	0
Saudi Arabia	2	Morocco	1
Morocco	1	Holland	2
Belgium	0	Saudi Arabia	1

	P	W	D	L	F	A	Pts
Holland	3	2	0	1	4	3	6
Saudi Arabia	3	2	0	1	4	3	6
Morocco	3	2	0	1	2	1	6
Belgium	3	0	0	3	2	5	0

SECOND ROUND

* After extra time

Germany	3	Belgium	2
Spain	3	Switzerland	0
Sweden	3	Saudi Arabia	1
Romania	3	Argentina	2
Holland	2	Rep of Ireland	0
Brazil	1	USA	0
Italy	2	Nigeria	1*
Bulgaria	1	Mexico	1*
(Bulgaria won 3-1 on pens)			

QUARTER-FINALS

* After extra time

Italy	2	Spain	1
Brazil	3	Holland	2
Bulgaria	2	Germany	1
Sweden	2	Romania	2*
(Sweden won 5-4 on pens)			

SEMI FINALS

Brazil	1	Sweden	0
Italy	2	Bulgaria	1

THIRD-PLACE MATCH

Sweden	4	Bulgaria	0

FINAL — JULY 17: ROSE BOWL, PASADENA

Brazil 0 **Italy 0** After extra time: Brazil 3-2 on pens

HT: 0-0. Att: 94,000. Puhl (Hungary)

Brazil: Taffarel - Jorginho (Cafu 20), Aldair, Marcio Santos, Branco - Mazinho (Viola 106), Dunga, Mauro Silva, Zinho - Romario, Bebeto.

Italy: Pagliuca - Mussi (Apolloni 34), Maldini, Baresi, Benarrivo – Donadoni, Berti, Albertini, D Baggio (Evani 94) - R Baggio, Massaro. **Top scorer:** 6 Salenko (Russia), Stoichkov (Bulgaria).

1994 USA

Awarding the finals to the United States upset football's purists but American fans responded with gusto. Record crowds thrilled to football vastly improved by a crackdown on cynical play. On the debit side, Argentine captain Diego Maradona was expelled after failing a dope test, Germany sent home their own Stefan Effenberg for a rude gesture to fans and Colombia's Andres Escobar was shot dead on returning home after scoring an own goal in a crucial first-round defeat by their American hosts. Brazil were deserved winners, inspired by Romario who scored five goals and claimed a hand in all their other six. However, Brazil owed victory to an unsatisfactory first-ever final shoot-out in which they beat Italy after a goalless draw, with star performer Roberto Baggio missing the decisive last spot-kick.

GROUP A

Brazil	2	Scotland	1
Morocco	2	Norway	2
Brazil	3	Morocco	0
Scotland	1	Norway	1
Brazil	1	Norway	2
Scotland	0	Morocco	3

	P	W	D	L	F	A	Pts
Brazil	3	2	0	1	6	3	6
Norway	3	1	2	0	5	4	5
Morocco	3	1	1	1	5	5	4
Scotland	3	0	1	2	2	6	1

GROUP B

Italy	2	Chile	2
Austria	1	Cameroon	1
Chile	1	Austria	1
Italy	3	Cameroon	0
Chile	1	Cameroon	1
Italy	2	Austria	1

	P	W	D	L	F	A	Pts
Italy	3	2	1	0	7	3	7
Chile	3	0	3	0	4	4	3
Austria	3	0	2	1	3	4	2
Cameroon	3	0	2	1	2	5	2

GROUP C

Saudi Arabia	0	Denmark	1
France	3	South Africa	0
France	4	Saudi Arabia	0
South Africa	1	Denmark	1
France	2	Denmark	1
South Africa	2	Saudi Arabia	2

	P	W	D	L	F	A	Pts
France	3	3	0	0	9	1	9
Denmark	3	1	1	1	3	3	4
S. Africa	3	0	2	1	3	6	2
S. Arabia	3	0	1	2	2	7	1

1998 FRANCE

GROUP D

Paraguay	0	Bulgaria	0
Spain	2	Nigeria	3
Nigeria	1	Bulgaria	0
Spain	0	Paraguay	0
Nigeria	1	Paraguay	3
Spain	6	Bulgaria	1

	P	W	D	L	F	A	Pts
Nigeria	3	2	0	1	5	5	6
Paraguay	3	1	2	0	3	1	5
Spain	3	1	1	1	8	4	4
Bulgaria	3	0	1	2	1	7	1

1998 FRANCE

World Cup history came full circle as France, whose Jules Rimet had instigated the tournament, won his prize for the first time in front of their own fans in the magnificent new Stade de France. Zinedine Zidane, the son of Algerian immigrants, recovered his nerve after a first-round red card and two-game ban, to head their crucial two first goals in the 3–0 final win over holders Brazil. Victory was a remarkable vindication of the French federation's academy system and the hard work of much-criticised coach Aime Jacquet. Croatia marked their debut at the finals by finishing third, while centre-forward Davor Suker ended up as the tournament's six-goal top scorer. England's dream ended in the second round after yet another shoot-out defeat, this time at the hands of Argentina. Manager Glenn Hoddle's men did well to last that long after young starlet David Beckham was sent off early in the second half. Consolation was the explosive form of World Cup new boy Michael Owen who stung the Argentines with the goal of the tournament.

QUARTER-FINALS

* After extra time

Italy	0	France	0*
(France won 4–3 on pens)			
Brazil	3	Denmark	2
Holland	2	Argentina	1
Germany	0	Croatia	3

GROUP E

South Korea	1	Mexico	3
Holland	0	Belgium	0
Belgium	2	Mexico	2
Holland	5	South Korea	0
Belgium	1	South Korea	1
Holland	2	Mexico	2

	P	W	D	L	F	A	Pts
Holland	3	1	2	0	7	2	5
Mexico	3	1	2	0	7	5	5
Belgium	3	0	3	0	3	3	3
S.Korea	3	0	1	2	2	9	1

GROUP G

England	2	Tunisia	0
Romania	1	Colombia	0
Colombia	1	Tunisia	0
Romania	2	England	1
Romania	1	Tunisia	1
Colombia	0	England	2

	P	W	D	L	F	A	Pts
Romania	3	2	1	0	4	2	7
England	3	2	0	1	5	2	6
Colombia	3	1	0	2	1	3	3
Tunisia	3	0	1	2	1	4	1

SECOND ROUND

* After extra time

Italy	1	Norway	0
Brazil	4	Chile	1
France	1	Paraguay	0*
(golden goal)			
Nigeria	1	Denmark	4
Germany	2	Mexico	1
Holland	2	Yugoslavia	1
Romania	0	Croatia	1
Argentina	2	England	2*
(Argentina won 4–3 on pens)			

SEMI FINALS

Brazil	1	Holland	1*
(Brazil won 4–2 on pens)			
France	2	Croatia	1

GROUP F

Germany	2	USA	0
Yugoslavia	1	Iran	0
Germany	2	Yugoslavia	2
USA	1	Iran	2
Germany	2	Iran	0
USA	0	Yugoslavia	1

	P	W	D	L	F	A	Pts
Germany	3	2	1	0	6	2	7
Yugoslavia	3	2	1	0	4	2	7
Iran	3	1	0	2	2	4	3
USA	3	0	0	3	1	5	0

GROUP H

Argentina	1	Japan	0
Jamaica	1	Croatia	3
Japan	0	Croatia	1
Argentina	5	Jamaica	0
Argentina	1	Croatia	0
Japan	1	Jamaica	2

	P	W	D	L	F	A	Pts
Argentina	3	3	0	0	7	0	9
Croatia	3	2	0	1	4	2	6
Jamaica	3	1	0	2	3	9	3
Japan	3	0	0	3	1	5	0

THIRD-PLACE MATCH

Holland	1	Croatia	2

FINAL — JULY 12: STADE DE FRANCE, SAINT-DENIS

France 3 (Zidane 27, 45, Petit 90)
Brazil 0
HT: 1-0. Att: 75,000. Ref: Belqola (Morocco)
France: Barthez - Thuram, Leboeuf, Desailly, Lizarazu-Petit, Deschamps, Karembeu (Boghossian 58), Zidane-Guivarc'h (Dugarry 66), Djorkaeff (Vieira 76). **Sent off:** Desailly.
Brazil: Taffarel - Cafu, Junior Baiano, Aldair, Roberto Carlos - Dunga, Cesar Sampaio (Edmundo 75), Leonardo (Denilson 46) - Rivaldo, Bebeto, Ronaldo.
Top scorer: 6 Suker (Croatia).

GROUP A

Senegal	1	France	0
Denmark	2	Uruguay	1
France	0	Uruguay	0
Denmark	1	Senegal	1
Denmark	2	France	0
Senegal	3	Uruguay	3

	P	W	D	L	F	A	Pts
Denmark	3	2	1	0	5	2	7
Senegal	3	1	2	0	5	4	5
Uruguay	3	0	2	1	4	5	2
France	3	0	1	2	0	3	1

GROUP D

South Korea	2	Poland	0
USA	3	Portugal	2
South Korea	1	USA	1
Portugal	4	Poland	0
South Korea	1	Portugal	0
Poland	3	USA	1

	P	W	D	L	F	A	Pts
South Korea	3	2	1	0	4	1	7
USA	3	1	1	1	5	6	4
Portugal	3	1	0	2	6	4	3
Poland	3	0	0	2	3	7	3

GROUP G

Mexico	1	Croatia	0
Italy	2	Ecuador	0
Croatia	2	Italy	1
Mexico	2	Ecuador	1
Mexico	1	Italy	1
Ecuador	1	Croatia	0

	P	W	D	L	F	A	Pts
Mexico	3	2	1	0	4	2	7
Italy	3	1	1	1	4	3	4
Croatia	3	1	0	2	2	3	3
Ecuador	3	1	0	2	2	4	3

SECOND ROUND

* After extra time

Germany	1	Paraguay	0
England	3	Denmark	0
Senegal	2	Sweden	1* (golden goal)
Spain	1	Rep.Ireland	1*
(Spain won 3–2 on pens)			
United States	2	Mexico	0
Brazil	2	Belgium	0
Turkey	1	Japan	0
South Korea	2	Italy	1*

SEMI FINALS

Germany	1	South Korea	0
Brazil	1	Turkey	0

GROUP B

Paraguay	2	South Africa	2
Spain	3	Slovenia	1
Spain	3	Paraguay	1
South Africa	1	Slovenia	0
Spain	3	South Africa	2
Paraguay	3	Slovenia	1

	P	W	D	L	F	A	Pts
Spain	3	3	0	0	9	4	9
Paraguay	3	1	1	1	6	6	4
South Africa	3	1	1	1	5	5	4
Slovenia	3	0	0	3	2	7	0

GROUP E

Rep. Ireland	1	Cameroon	1
Germany	8	Saudi Arabia	0
Germany	1	Rep. Ireland	1
Cameroon	1	Saudi Arabia	0
Germany	2	Cameroon	0
Rep. Ireland	3	Saudi Arabia	0

	P	W	D	L	F	A	Pts
Germany	3	2	1	0	11	1	7
Rep. Ireland	3	1	2	0	5	2	5
Cameroon	3	1	1	1	2	3	4
Saudi Arabia	3	0	0	3	0	12	0

GROUP H

Japan	2	Belgium	2
Russia	2	Tunisia	0
Japan	1	Russia	0
Tunisia	1	Belgium	1
Japan	2	Tunisia	0
Belgium	3	Russia	2

	P	W	D	L	F	A	Pts
Japan	3	2	1	0	5	2	7
Belgium	3	1	2	0	6	5	5
Russia	3	1	0	2	4	4	3
Tunisia	3	0	1	2	1	5	1

QUARTER-FINALS

* After extra time

Brazil	2	England	1
Germany	1	United States	0
South Korea	0	Spain	0*
(Korea won 5–4 on pens)			
Turkey	1	Senegal	0* (golden goal)

GROUP C

Brazil	2	Turkey	1
Costa Rica	2	China	0
Brazil	4	China	0
Costa Rica	1	Turkey	1
Brazil	5	Costa Rica	2
Turkey	3	China	0

	P	W	D	L	F	A	Pts
Brazil	3	3	0	0	11	3	9
Turkey	3	1	1	1	5	3	4
Costa Rica	3	1	1	1	5	6	4
China	3	0	0	3	0	9	0

GROUP F

England	1	Sweden	1
Argentina	1	Nigeria	0
Sweden	2	Nigeria	1
England	1	Argentina	0
Sweden	1	Argentina	1
Nigeria	0	England	0

	P	W	D	L	F	A	Pts
Sweden	3	1	2	0	4	3	5
England	3	1	2	0	2	1	5
Argentina	3	1	1	1	2	2	4
Nigeria	3	0	1	2	1	3	1

2002 S.KOREA/JAPAN

Ronaldo made amends for the 1998 upset by leading Brazil to arecord-extending fifth World Cup win. Japan and South Korea shared the honour of hosting the first finals staged in Asia and the first to be co-hosted. Japan reached the second round, while the Koreans, under Dutch coach Guus Hiddink, reached the semi-finals before losing to Germany. By contrast, fatigue born of the ever-more-stressful club season took a heavy toll on Europe's giants. Holders France collapsed in the first round without scoring a goal, Italy fell in the second round on a golden goal to the Koreans, while England tottered to a quarter-final standstill against Brazil. Ronaldinho scored a freakish winning goal before being sent off but returned, refreshed, for the 2–0 final defeat of the Germans. Ronaldo struck both goals and was the event's eight-goal top scorer.

THIRD-PLACE MATCH

Turkey	3	South Korea	2

FINAL — JUNE 30: INTERNATIONAL, YOKOHAMA

Brazil 2 (Ronaldo 68, 79) **Germany 0**
HT: 0-0. Att: 69,029. Ref: Collina (Italy)
Brazil: Marcos - Cafu, Lucio, Roque Junior, Edmilson, Roberto Carlos - Gilberto Silva, Kleberson - Ronaldinho (Juninho 85), Ronaldo (Denilson 90), Rivaldo.
Germany: Kahn - Linke, Ramelow, Metzelder, Bode (Ziege 84) - Schneider, Frings, Hamann, Jeremies (Asamoah 78) - Neuville, Klose (Bierhoff 74). **Top scorer:** 8 Ronaldo (Brazil).

WORLD CUP SCORECHART

GROUP A

Date	Time	Venue	Home			Away
09-JUN-06	1700 BST	MUNICH	GERMANY			COSTA RICA
09-JUN-06	2000 BST	GELSENKIRCHEN	POLAND			ECUADOR
14-JUN-06	2000 BST	DORTMUND	GERMANY			POLAND
15-JUN-06	1400 BST	HAMBURG	ECUADOR			COSTA RICA
20-JUN-06	1500 BST	BERLIN	ECUADOR			GERMANY
20-JUN-06	1500 BST	HANOVER	COSTA RICA			POLAND

GROUP B

Date	Time	Venue	Home			Away
10-JUN-06	1400 BST	FRANKFURT	ENGLAND			PARAGUAY
10-JUN-06	1700 BST	DORTMUND	TRINIDAD&TOBAGO			SWEDEN
15-JUN-06	1700 BST	NUREMBERG	ENGLAND			TRINIDAD&TOBAGO
15-JUN-06	2000 BST	BERLIN	SWEDEN			PARAGUAY
20-JUN-06	2000 BST	KAISERSLAUTERN	PARAGUAY			TRINIDAD&TOBAGO
20-JUN-06	2000 BST	COLOGNE	SWEDEN			ENGLAND

GROUP E

Date	Time	Venue	Home			Away
12-JUN-06	1700 BST	GELSENKIRCHEN	USA			CZECH REPUBLIC
12-JUN-06	2000 BST	HANOVER	ITALY			GHANA
17-JUN-06	2000 BST	KAISERSLAUTERN	ITALY			USA
17-JUN-06	1700 BST	COLOGNE	CZECH REPUBLIC			GHANA
22-JUN-06	1500 BST	HAMBURG	CZECH REPUBLIC			ITALY
22-JUN-06	1500 BST	NUREMBERG	GHANA			USA

GROUP F

Date	Time	Venue	Home			Away
12-JUN-06	1400 BST	KAISERSLAUTERN	AUSTRALIA			JAPAN
13-JUN-06	2000 BST	BERLIN	BRAZIL			CROATIA
18-JUN-06	1400 BST	NUREMBERG	JAPAN			CROATIA
18-JUN-06	1700 BST	MUNICH	BRAZIL			AUSTRALIA
22-JUN-06	2000 BST	DORTMUND	JAPAN			BRAZIL
22-JUN-06	2000 BST	STUTTGART	CROATIA			AUSTRALIA

SECOND ROUND

Match	Date	Time	Venue	Home			Away
1	24-JUN-06	1600 BST	MUNICH	WINNER A			RUNNER UP B
2	24-JUN-06	2000 BST	LEIPZIG	WINNER C			RUNNER UP D
3	25-JUN-06	1600 BST	STUTTGART	WINNER B			RUNNER UP A
4	25-JUN-06	2000 BST	NUREMBERG	WINNER D			RUNNER UP C
5	26-JUN-06	1600 BST	KAISERSLAUTERN	WINNER E			RUNNER UP F
6	26-JUN-06	2000 BST	COLOGNE	WINNER G			RUNNER UP H
7	27-JUN-06	1600 BST	DORTMUND	WINNER F			RUNNER UP E
8	27-JUN-06	2000 BST	HANOVER	WINNER H			RUNNER UP G

FINAL 2006

Match	Date	Time	Venue	Home			Away
3	9-JUL-06	1900 BST	BERLIN	WINNER SF 1			WINNER SF 2

GROUP C

Date	Time	Venue	Team 1			Team 2
10-JUN-06	2000 BST	HAMBURG	ARGENTINA			IVORY COAST
11-JUN-06	1400 BST	LEIPZIG	SERBIA			HOLLAND
16-JUN-06	1400 BST	GELSENKIRCHEN	ARGENTINA			SERBIA
16-JUN-06	1700 BST	STUTTGART	HOLLAND			IVORY COAST
21-JUN-06	2000 BST	FRANKFURT	HOLLAND			ARGENTINA
21-JUN-06	2000 BST	MUNICH	IVORY COAST			SERBIA

GROUP D

Date	Time	Venue	Team 1			Team 2
11-JUN-06	1700 BST	NUREMBERG	MEXICO			IRAN
11-JUN-06	2000 BST	COLOGNE	ANGOLA			PORTUGAL
16-JUN-06	2000 BST	HANOVER	MEXICO			ANGOLA
17-JUN-06	1400 BST	FRANKFURT	PORTUGAL			IRAN
21-JUN-06	1500 BST	GELSENKIRCHEN	PORTUGAL			MEXICO
21-JUN-06	1500 BST	LEIPZIG	IRAN			ANGOLA

GROUP G

Date	Time	Venue	Team 1			Team 2
13-JUN-06	1400 BST	FRANKFURT	SOUTH KOREA			TOGO
13-JUN-06	1700 BST	STUTTGART	FRANCE			SWITZERLAND
18-JUN-06	2000 BST	LEIPZIG	FRANCE			SOUTH KOREA
19-JUN-06	1400 BST	DORTMUND	TOGO			SWITZERLAND
23-JUN-06	2000 BST	HANOVER	SWITZERLAND			SOUTH KOREA
23-JUN-06	2000 BST	COLOGNE	TOGO			FRANCE

GROUP H

Date	Time	Venue	Team 1			Team 2
14-JUN-06	1400 BST	LEIPZIG	SPAIN			UKRAINE
14-JUN-06	1700 BST	MUNICH	TUNISIA			SAUDI ARABIA
19-JUN-06	1700 BST	HAMBURG	SAUDI ARABIA			UKRAINE
19-JUN-06	2000 BST	STUTTGART	SPAIN			TUNISIA
23-JUN-06	1500 BST	BERLIN	UKRAINE			TUNISIA
23-JUN-06	1500 BST	KAISERSLAUTERN	SAUDI ARABIA			SPAIN

QUARTER FINALS

	Date	Time	Venue			
A	30-JUN-06	1600 BST	BERLIN	WINNER MATCH 1		WINNER MATCH 2
B	30-JUN-06	2000 BST	HAMBURG	WINNER MATCH 5		WINNER MATCH 6
C	01-JUL-06	1600 BST	GELSENKIRCHEN	WINNER MATCH 3		WINNER MATCH 4
D	01-JUL-06	2000 BST	FRANKFURT	WINNER MATCH 7		WINNER MATCH 8

SEMI FINALS

	Date	Time	Venue			
1	04-JUL-06	2000 BST	DORTMUND	WINNER QF A		WINNER QF B
2	05-JUL-06	2000 BST	MUNICH	WINNER QF C		WINNER QF D

THIRD PLACE MATCH

Date	Time	Venue			
08-JUL-06	2000 BST	STUTTGART	LOSER 1		LOSER 2

WINNER 2006

TEAM	LINE-UP

ACKNOWLEDGEMENTS

Thanks to Kevin Connolly and Andrew Warshaw for their assistance with the text

The publishers would like to thank the following sources for their kind permission to reproduce the pictures in this book. The page numbers for each of the photographs are listed below, giving the page on which they appear in the book. Any location indicator (t-top, b-bottom, l-left, r-right).

Empics: /Frank Augstein/AP: 33b, /Greg Baker/AP: 40, /Oliver Berg/AP: 12tl, /Armando Franca/AP: 43r, 51t, /Riccardo Gangale/AP: 17, /Rob Griffith/AP: 14, /Petr David Josek/AP: 49r, /Thomas Kienzle/AP: 2, 8, /Kai Uwe Knoth/AP: 21b, /Dmitry Lovetsky/AP: 44, /Jens Meyer/AP: 1, /Roberto Pfeil/AP: 6, /Natacha Pisarenko/AP: 33t, /Michael Probst/AP: 51b, /Hans Punz/AP: 63b, /Eckehard Schulz/AP: 9, /Murad Sezer/AP: 58, /Alexander Zemlianichenko/AP: 42, /Simon Bellis: 26, 27r, /Jon Buckle: 18, 31b, 41, 53, 53r, 54, 63t, /Sergei Chuzavkov: 65l, /Barry Coombs: 37t, /DPA: 70, 80, /Adam Davy: 4-5, 29, 46, /Mike Egerton: 23l, 27l, /Nigel French: 22, 59l, /Efrem Lukatsky: 65r, /Mario Castillo/Jam Media: 39b, /Tony Marshall: 15b, 19, 21t, 24, 25, 34, 37b, 43r, 45b, 57t, 59r, 60, /Michael Reagan: 15t, 23r, 35, 61, /Neal Simpson: 12tr, 38, 50, 66, 67, /Steve Welsh/PA: 45t, /John Walton: 20, 30, 31t, 32, 36, 39t, 47, 48, 49r, 52, 55, 56, 57b, /Paul White: 62.

Getty Images: /STR/AFP: 28.

Offside/L'Equipe: 12 bl, /Witters: 10t, 10b, 11t, 11bl, 11br, 12br, 13tl, 13tr, 13b.

Every effort has been made to acknowledge correctly and contact the source and/or copyright holder of each picture and Carlton Books Limited apologises for any unintentional errors or omissions, which will be corrected in future editions of this book.